Lois Lowry

WHO WROTE THAT?

WHO WROTE THAT?

Lowis Lowry

John Bankston

Foreword by
Kyle Zimmer

Severna Park
Middle School
Media Center

CHELSEA HOUSE
PUBLISHERS
An imprint of Infobase Publishing

Lois Lowry

Chelsea House
An imprint of Infobase Publishing
132 West 31st Street
New York NY 10001

Library of Congress Cataloging-in-Publication Data
Bankston, John, 1974-
 Lois Lowry / John Bankston.
 p. cm. — (Who wrote that?)
 Includes bibliographical references and index.
 ISBN 978-1-60413-335-6
 1. Lowry, Lois—Criticism and interpretation. 2. Authors, American—20th century—Biography—Juvenile literature. 3. Children's stories—Authorship—Juvenile literature. 4. Young adult fiction—Authorship—Juvenile literature.
 I. Title. II. Series.
 PS3562.O923Z59 2009
 813'.54—dc22
 [B]   2008035039

Table of Contents

FOREWORD BY
KYLE ZIMMER
PRESIDENT, FIRST BOOK

HUMANITY IS POWERED by stories. From our earliest days as thinking beings, we employed every available tool to tell each other stories. We danced, drew pictures on the walls of our caves, spoke, and sang. All of this extraordinary effort was designed to entertain, recount the news of the day, explain natural occurrences—and then gradually to build religious and cultural traditions and establish the common bonds and continuity that eventually formed civilizations. Stories are the most powerful force in the universe; they are the primary element that has distinguished our evolutionary path.

Our love of the story has not diminished with time. Enormous segments of societies are devoted to the art of storytelling. Book sales in the United States alone topped $24 billion in 2006; movie studios spend fortunes to create and promote stories; and the news industry is more pervasive in its presence than ever before.

There is no mystery to our fascination. Great stories are magic. They can introduce us to new cultures, or remind us of the nobility and failures of our own, inspire us to greatness or scare us to death; but above all, stories provide human insight on a level that is unavailable through any other source. In fact, stories connect each of us to the rest of humanity not just in our own time, but also throughout history.

This special magic of books is the greatest treasure that we can hand down from generation to generation. In fact, that spark in a child that comes from books became the motivation for the creation of my organization, First Book, a national literacy program with a simple mission: to provide new books to the most disadvantaged children. At present, First Book has been at work in hundreds of communities for over a decade. Every year children in need receive millions of books through our organization and millions more are provided through dedicated literacy institutions across the United States and around the world. In addition, groups of people dedicate themselves tirelessly to working with children to share reading and stories in every imaginable setting from schools to the streets. Of course, this Herculean effort serves many important goals. Literacy translates to productivity and employability in life and many other valid and even essential elements. But at the heart of this movement are people who love stories, love to read, and want desperately to ensure that no one misses the wonderful possibilities that reading provides.

When thinking about the importance of books, there is an overwhelming urge to cite the literary devotion of great minds. Some have written of the magnitude of the importance of literature. Amy Lowell, an American poet, captured the concept when she said, "Books are more than books. They are the life, the very heart and core of ages past, the reason why men lived and worked and died, the essence and quintessence of their lives." Others have spoken of their personal obsession with books, as in Thomas Jefferson's simple statement: "I live for books." But more compelling, perhaps, is the almost instinctive excitement in children for books and stories.

Throughout my years at First Book, I have heard truly extraordinary stories about the power of books in the lives of children. In one case, a homeless child, who had been bounced from one location to another, later resurfaced—and the only possession that he had fought to keep was the book he was given as part of a First Book distribution months earlier. More recently, I met a child who, upon receiving the book he wanted, flashed a big smile and said, "This is my big chance!" These snapshots reveal the true power of books and stories to give hope and change lives.

As these children grow up and continue to develop their love of reading, they will owe a profound debt to those volunteers who reached out to them—a debt that they may repay by reaching out to spark the next generation of readers. But there is a greater debt owed by all of us—a debt to the storytellers, the authors, who have bound us together, inspired our leaders, fueled our civilizations, and helped us put our children to sleep with their heads full of images and ideas.

WHO WROTE THAT? is a series of books dedicated to introducing us to a few of these incredible individuals. While we have almost always honored stories, we have not uniformly honored storytellers. In fact, some of the most important authors have toiled in complete obscurity throughout their lives or have been openly persecuted for the uncomfortable truths that they have laid before us. When confronted with the magnitude of their written work or perhaps the daily grind of our own, we can forget that writers are people. They struggle through the same daily indignities and dental appointments, and they experience the intense joy and bottomless despair that many of us do. Yet somehow they rise above it all to deliver a powerful thread that connects us all. It is a rare honor to have the opportunity that these books provide to share the lives of these extraordinary people. Enjoy.

Lois Lowry, in a recent photo taken in front of her home.

The Rest of My Life

LOOKING AT THE eighth graders in front of her, Lois Lowry took a deep breath. They were restless and sweating. Those who were not fidgeting looked ready to fall asleep. None of them were there for Lowry's speech. They were there to graduate.

It was a humid June day in 1978. Dressed up in suits and skirts, the kids looked as uncomfortable as Lowry felt. She had listened while their principal told them that these were their golden years and she had watched as the students grew bored while their superintendent compared life to a football game.

Above, Luke Skywalker (played by Mark Hamill) and his Jedi master, Yoda (voiced by Frank Oz), in the second Star Wars *film,* The Empire Strikes Back. *After reading Joseph Campbell's* The Hero with a Thousand Faces, *George Lucas revised his film trilogy to better suit the kind of hero's journey described in Campbell's book.*

Approaching the podium, Lowry looked at the first rows of kids on the stage and then to their parents, teachers, and relatives seated in the middle school's gym. She did not have a speech ready. Her first novel, *A Summer to Die*, had just been published, and that spring, she had won the International Reading Association's Children's Literature Award. That came with a prize of $1,000—four times what she had earned the month before. She was 41 years old. *What* could she possibly tell a group of restless teens about their future?

"By now the kids were almost falling asleep, they were so hot and so bored," Lowry recalled in a speech to the National Council of Teachers of English convention nearly 20 years later. "I said that I was sorry, but I didn't think these were their golden years at all. I thought that if you had to assign a color to eighth grade—based on my own memories, I would assign it dull beige. At best, dull

Did you know...

Director George Lucas had written two drafts of *Star Wars* before discovering that Joseph Campbell's *The Hero with a Thousand Faces* provided a template for his screenplay. He used the book when he rewrote the script—it made it easier to view the challenges of the universe from the perspective of a single person. Since then, numerous filmmakers (including the creators of *The Matrix* trilogy) have recognized how Campbell's examination of a hero's journey progresses like a movie: The main character overcomes challenges, emerging stronger and wiser at the end.

beige. *Golden*, I told them, comes later, if it ever comes at all."[1]

Life was not a football game, either. She was sure of that. Football is a sport with clear rules and penalties, and, most important, "several guys in striped shirts"—referees—are paid to keep track of everything. When the rules are broken, there are almost always immediate consequences. "Life is much more of a complicated set of surprises, and when you need the striped-shirt guys, they are nowhere in sight; and often there is no one who cheers if you make a good block. And there is frequently no team—you're just out on the field all alone."

It was a short speech. When she was done, the author looked around. The eighth grade class was no longer bored. They were grinning, and a few nudged their peers in recognition. Lowry recalled,

> They were looking at me as if I knew what I was talking about, but then I looked out into the gymnasium, at all the parents and grandparents, and their faces were like concrete. I realized in that moment that I could talk to the kids—or I could talk to the parents—but I couldn't talk to both at the same time, not with any truth, not without platitudes. And so I chose the kids. It was a moment of epiphany.[2]

ON A JOURNEY

According to the dictionary, an epiphany can be "an intuitive grasp of reality through something (as an event) usually simple and striking," such as Lowry observing the contrast between the adults in her audience and the teens and knowing immediately the direction her life would take. In her writing, a character's epiphany is just as important—it means "an illuminating discovery, realization, or disclosure: a revealing scene or moment."[3]

Joseph Campbell was an American professor who devoted his professional life to the study of comparative religion and mythology. All over the world, he saw similar themes in fairy tales and Greek mythology, the spoken word stories of Native American spirit guides, and modern movies. Campbell's description of a spiritual quest is similar to an epiphany: "The quest to find the inward thing that you basically are."[4]

Lois Lowry has spent her life doing just that. Her quest clarified in that stuffy gym, she realized who she was and what she wanted to do with the rest of her life. Later, after two decades of writing for young adults, she came to one vital conclusion: "A journey is a way of figuring out what stuff matters, and of getting rid of what doesn't."[5]

Nearly every story describes a journey. Plays, movies, novels, and even some poems depict the quest of the main character, or protagonist. Journeys can be internal: The protagonist might cope with an emotional struggle—a parent's divorce, a new sibling, or freshman year at an unfamiliar school.

In Lowry's first published novel, *A Summer to Die*, the main character, Meg, copes with her family's sudden move to a rural area and having to share space with her older sister for the first time: "Molly is fifteen," Meg explains, "which means that she puts on eye shadow when Mom doesn't catch her at it, and she spends hours in front of the mirror arranging her hair different ways . . . and she talks on the phone every evening to friends, mostly about boys."[6] As her sister battles a mysterious illness, Meg draws comfort from a neighbor in his 70s and her love for photography. Much of the book deals with her inner journey as she learns what is important and to value her gifts.

A journey can also be external, focused on what happens in the outside world and not just inside the main character's head. Often in these stories, the hero (and heroes, of course, can be male or female) travels toward a destination.

Journeys can also be *both* internal and external. In Lowry's best-known work, *The Giver*, the journey of protagonist Jonas begins when he questions the society he was born into. His internal struggles represent a journey away from his comfortable childhood acceptance of his life and toward skeptical adulthood as he questions his society's values. This internal struggle culminates with a physical journey as Jonas flees his village.

MAKING CHOICES

Heroes are defined by their choices: Actions speak louder than words. As Joseph Campbell explained to interviewer Bill Moyers,

> There are two types of deed. One is the physical deed, in which the hero performs a courageous act in battle or saves a life. The other kind is the spiritual deed, in which the hero learns to experience the supernormal range of human spiritual life and then comes back with a message.[7]

Lois Lowry's personal struggles and the choices she made might not have been as dramatic as Jonas's, but the challenges she faced offer inspiration to both aspiring writers and her millions of readers.

Novels and movies are stories about the main character's journey, as are biographies. Lowry's epiphany was an important moment, but it came well into her adulthood. Her journey began as most biographies do, at the beginning: She was born just a few years before the United States was plunged into the worst war the world has ever known.

"December 7, 1941—a date which will live in infamy." The Japanese attack on the American naval base at Pearl Harbor not only brought the United States into World War II, but also changed the life of the author, who as a young girl would see her father, Major Robert Hammersberg, go off to war.

2

Optical Allusions

IN A MOVIE, a young girl struggles with a sunbonnet. She giggles as the ocean breeze gusts, tossing her blonde hair. With one hand she clamps the hat to her head. With the other she clutches a shovel, preparing to dig a hole along the Waikiki shoreline. An indistinct shape looms behind her. It seems almost ominous.

The girl was Lois Lowry, age three. Today many people have their own video cameras, but almost 70 years ago, few owned movie cameras. Major Robert Hammersberg was one of those who did, and footage that he shot has survived the decades.

Much of it is in color, depicting his family and the lush island paradise where they lived.

In one of these home movies, his daughter can be seen playing in the foreground. In the background, a shadow obscures the horizon. For years Lowry assumed it was another island. It was not. Examined more closely, the shape, although "hidden, shrouded and obscured, floating in that idyllic, still-blue sea," was a ship that held 1,200 men, Lowry later recalled. "They would all be dead soon."[1]

In the 1930s, Hawaii was a territory of the United States; it would not be granted statehood until 1959. A chain of islands more than 1,000 miles long, it is almost 2,390 miles from California and 4,900 miles from Japan. It was also home to the Pearl Harbor Naval Base. The base's ships and planes provided protection for the mainland.

It was in Hawaii that Major Hammersberg and his wife, Katherine, were raising a family. The couple already had a daughter, Helen, when Cena Ericson Hammersberg

Did you know...

Hawaii was a monarchy until 1893. On April 30, 2008, protesters seized the Iolani Palace and demanded that Hawaii be returned to its royal roots and cede from the United States. Although it has supporters, this movement is unlikely to succeed.

was born on March 20, 1937. The baby was named for Robert's mother, but the major's mother did not want the honor. "I think that was true so often of immigrants," Lowry explained. "They wanted their children and then their grandchildren to be very American." Cena's name was changed a few weeks later to a much more American one: Lois Ann.[2]

> I am glad that I was born on the island of Oahu, so that my first memories, have been of rainbows and the scent of flowers—that those things became part of the earliest part of me. I have over the years so many times told friends—and family—that I remembered being barefoot on the beach there—barely walking, so young—with that warm blue water beside me.[3]

This blissful life and that of her family was about to be affected by the choices of leaders thousands of miles away.

WORLD EVENTS

Adolf Hitler had consolidated power in Germany, and, by the end of the 1930s, his plan for the Nazi army to control Europe, and eventually the world, was in full swing. On September 1, 1939, his army invaded Poland, which soon fell to the superior German forces. The action prompted both France and Great Britain to declare war two days later.

German forces then invaded Belgium, Holland, and eventually France. In 1941, Hitler's army invaded Russia, even as German forces continued their air assaults against Great Britain, devastating cities such as London. The German Axis was joined by Italy and Japan, but American involvement in these conflicts was minimal.

The United States had entered the Great Depression with the stock market crash of 1929. Unemployment in some regions soared to 25 percent: One out of four adults who wanted a job could not find one. Mass migration from devastated dust bowl communities in Oklahoma and other farm states, bank failures, rampant poverty—all were issues that President Franklin Delano Roosevelt and Congress dealt with from his election in 1932 through the rest of the decade. The United States had little interest, or the resources, to wage war thousands of miles away. The choice not to fight was eliminated at dawn on December 7, 1941.

Flying in tight formation, more than 350 Japanese aircraft barraged the unprepared naval base at Pearl Harbor in Hawaii with withering fire. Before it was over, 2,388 military personal were killed and much of the U.S. Pacific Fleet was in ruins. The next day, in a speech to congress, Roosevelt described the battle in this way:

> [A] date which will live in infamy—the United States of America was suddenly and deliberately attacked by naval and air forces of the Empire of Japan. The United States was at peace with that nation, and, at the solicitation of Japan, was still in conversation with its government and its emperor looking toward the maintenance of peace in the Pacific. . . . It will be recorded that the distance of Hawaii from Japan makes it obvious that the attack was deliberately planned many days or even weeks ago. During the intervening time the Japanese government has deliberately sought to deceive the United States by false statements and expressions of hope for continued peace. The attack yesterday on the Hawaiian Islands has caused severe damage to American naval and military forces. I regret to tell you that very many American lives have been lost. In addition, American ships have been reported torpedoed

on the high seas between San Francisco and Honolulu. Yesterday the Japanese government also launched an attack against Malaya. Last night Japanese forces attacked Hong Kong. Last night Japanese forces attacked Guam. Last night Japanese forces attacked the Philippine Islands. Last night Japanese forces attacked Wake Island. And this morning the Japanese attacked Midway Island. Japan has, therefore, undertaken a surprise offensive extending throughout the Pacific area. The facts of yesterday and today speak for themselves. . . . As commander in chief of the Army and Navy I have directed that all measures be taken for our defense.[4]

This was considered an act of war. Soon, the United States military was fighting opposing armies on the continents of Asia, Europe, and even Africa.

GROWING UP

Not long after she appeared in those home movies, Lois and her family moved to New York. Her sister began to attend school, and she remembers having a precious secret. Her sister, playing teacher, had started the process: On her own, young Lois—barely four—could read simple books by herself. Reading is not her clearest memory from that time, however: "We were in New York when Pearl Harbor was attacked," Lowry recalled, "and that's actually one of my early memories, seeing my parents' reaction to that news."[5]

Major Hammersberg was the photographer of the family. Those who take pictures rarely appear in them, but Lowry remembers one exception. "After the radio said, 'Pearl Harbor,' and my mother cried, my father set up his camera one day, sat in front of it with the magical button in his hand, and took his own picture," Lowry recalled nearly six decades later. "The picture my father took of himself in 1941 haunts me today. He looks sad in it. He looks pensive, and tired, and perhaps angry at what is happening to him and the world. At the same time, I can see in that picture the gentle eyes that I remember."[6]

Decades later, Lowry had her father's old movies converted to videotape. Watching the footage with friends, one commented on a shape in the background. "Are you sure that was Waikiki? *The beach scene?* Are you sure it was Honolulu? It didn't look like it to me," the friend said, explaining, "There's an island. And if you stand on the beach at Waikiki, there are no islands in the distance."

Lowry was sure it was Waikiki; she rewound and froze the image. "My friend John, a former Naval officer once stationed in Honolulu looked carefully," Lowry remembered. "'It's a ship,' he said at last, after we re-ran the tape several times. 'It's a battleship. I think it might be the *Arizona*,' he said. A silence fell in my living room."[7]

The *Arizona* had been sunk by Japanese aircraft in the attack on Pearl Harbor. Almost everyone on board died. The act of war sent Lowry's father into the Pacific in 1942 and the rest of the family into Katherine's parents' home in Pennsylvania. What was revealed in the videotape prompted Lowry to dig even deeper in her writing.

"I think, as adults looking at childhood, we tend to see the child playing in the sand: the scene that makes us say 'ahhhhhhh' with a sense of nostalgia," she said in a speech at Brown University in early 2001. "Perhaps we need to look more carefully—more honestly—at what floats there on the horizon."[8]

Many cars have etched on their passenger side mirror: "Objects are closer than they appear." If a saying was

Major Robert Hammersberg's self-portrait, taken shortly after the attack on Pearl Harbor.

affixed to Lowry's later novels, it might read, "*Nothing* is as it appears."

In *Gathering Blue*, the middle title of the trilogy that began with *The Giver*, the main character is nine-year-old Kira. In the beginning of the story, her mother dies. Her father died years earlier, and she is now an orphan. In her primitive village, this jeopardizes Kira's life. From Lowry's Web site, the novel is described as a "speculation on the nature of the future of human society, life in Kira's community is nasty, brutish, and for the ill or disabled, short."[9]

After Kira is rescued by The Guardians, her life seems blessed. Once getting enough to eat was a serious worry; now she feasts three times a day. No longer does she have to bathe in a stream; now she enjoys hot and cold running water in a bathtub, whose function must be explained to her. The only rule seems to be that she must contribute her talent. She has an amazing gift for sewing, and the robe that belongs to the mystical Singer must be repaired.

As Kira looks closer at the others who are kept by The Guardians, however, she realizes that their lives are far from perfect. "At the conclusion of *Gathering Blue*," Lowry later explained, "it is a child—a young girl—who holds in her hands the power and determination to change a world brutalized by evil."[10] Kira's determination arrives after exploring her new home and discovering a child who has been kidnapped.

A NEW HOME

In 1942, Lois Lowry had a new home to explore as well. Following her father's deployment, she and her family moved to Carlisle, Pennsylvania, to live with Lowry's grandparents. Her older sister was in elementary school and making new friends, and her mother was busy with Lois's younger brother, Jonathon, a baby she was trying to keep quiet. Lowry remembers that the baby's crying made her grandmother "very, very nervous. A lot of things made my grandmother very, very nervous," Lowry later admitted, "and I seemed to be one of them: my messiness, my carelessness."[11]

Lowry did her best to keep out of everyone's way. Her grandparents' cook showed the little girl the servants' stairs, a hidden passageway unknown to most of her family. Using it, she could disappear in one part of the house and reappear in another. She could use her imagination—sometimes to scare herself. In addition to the secret staircase, the home's book-lined library was an ideal environment for the future author.

Lowry has admitted that, as a young girl, she was a bit of a liar. Her grandfather used to read William Cullen Bryant's "Thanatopsis," a long and complicated poem, aloud to his granddaughters. Her older sister had no problem calling it boring and leaving the room. Eight-year-old Helen preferred to share the plots from Nancy Drew novels with him, something the grandfather found boring.

Five-year-old Lois told a white lie: She said she liked the poem! As her younger brother was just a baby, the middle child quickly became grandfather's favorite. Every afternoon, she curled up in her grandfather's lap and he would ask her what she wanted to hear. Every afternoon she would ask for the poem featuring "the speechless babe, and the gray-headed man."

Little Lois was certain that the line described them. Maybe because of that, or because of the older man's joy in reading it to her, she never varied her request. While her baby brother napped and her sister played, Lois would listen. One day her grandfather noticed her lips moving. "Are you reading that?" he asked.

"No. I can't read yet," Lois replied.[12] This wasn't completely true, of course. By then Lois could read—simple books, not the complex Victorian poem her grandfather enjoyed every afternoon. He covered the page, and she recited the next part. Without even trying, she had memorized it.

A few days later, her grandparents held a party. The children were asleep when Lois's grandfather crept into her room and gently shook her awake. He led the bleary-eyed child downstairs. Barefoot and in pink pajamas, she was brought before a group of unfamiliar adults. Her grandfather asked Lois to recite *Thanatopsis*. Other children might have frozen in fear. Lois did not. Quietly she recited the entire poem. At its conclusion, everyone clapped. Clearly she heard one man's review: "Amazing." Her performance would later alter her life's direction, and Lois's gift for public speaking never faded. Fiction authors are storytellers, but most are far more comfortable writing their stories than actually telling them.

A WRITER'S BEGINNINGS

Lois's love for reading came from her grandparents, her parents, and even her older sister. There was a time, though, when reading terrified her. In 1944, her father was stationed in the Pacific. He was not a soldier, but even being a dentist in a combat zone held tremendous risks. It was a dangerous place in a very dangerous time. "The huge headlines in our small-town newspaper scared me," she remembered. Her teacher, Louise Heckerman, "didn't tell me to cover my eyes. She told me to read. And she told me what to read, and how to talk about it, and where to find comfort in words."[13]

Lowry skipped the second grade. By then the future author was not just reading. "I was always writing," she remembers, "but when I was a child in elementary school, the creative arts were not given much attention, and I don't recall that we were ever called upon to do creative writing in school. It was something I did on my own."[14]

The war in the Pacific turned in America's favor after the U.S. victory at Midway in June 1942. The next year, Germany suffered its first major defeat when its army was routed by Russian forces at Stalingrad. Italy surrendered soon after. After the D-Day landings on the French beaches of Normandy in June 1944, Allied victories across Europe led to Germany's surrender in 1945. Japan surrendered on August 14, 1945, after the United States dropped atomic bombs on the cities of Hiroshima and Nagasaki. World War II had come to an end.

The United States military was instrumental in Japan's reconstruction, and its efforts helped Japan become a major U.S. ally. Lois's father moved to Tokyo and aided the reconstruction effort, and, in 1948, the rest of the family joined him. "We live in an American style house, with American neighbors," Lowry remembered in a speech to the group Children's Literature New England, "and our little community has its own movie theatre, which shows American movies; and a small church, a tiny library, and an elementary school; and in many ways it is an odd replica of a United States Village.

"At eleven years old, I am not a particularly adventurous child, nor am I a rebellious one. But I have always

Lois in Japan in 1949, with two of her family's maids. Lois and her family lived there while her father was stationed in postwar Tokyo during the reconstruction.

been curious."[15] Without telling her parents, Lowry passed through the gates of her village and entered the heart of Tokyo's Shibuya district. It was a noisy and even dangerous place. She rode past a Japanese elementary school, leaning against the fence and watching the children play. "But I never talk to anyone," she remembered. "I am not frightened of the people, who are so different than me, but I am shy."[16]

Well before then, she had used her observations to fashion stories. Once, a graduate student sent her a copy of something from her childhood:

> [It was] a letter that I wrote to a children's magazine in 1947, when I was ten and that letter described myself—as published in that magazine—says, "I am writing a book called, *A Dog Called Lucky*. I am on Chapter Thirteen." I have no memory of that, but I don't think I made it up. It was the kind of thing I was doing all the time—writing stories, writing what I thought of as books, in my little childhood notebooks. Also I used to write stories for my little brother, who was six years younger.[17]

Lowry kept her stories and her poems—all of her writing—in secret notebooks that she never showed to anyone. She envies children today who have the advantages of creative writing classes and can share their stories, but she knows that, even with that advantage, most of her scribbling would have stayed private. She thinks that every writer, but especially beginning writers, need that space to make mistakes and experiment.

Although she would write some of the stories longhand, eventually she took to composing them on her father's typewriter. He must have noticed, because for her thirteenth birthday he gave her a special present: a Smith-Corona typewriter. Lois's name was engraved on the carrying case. Today, many kids have their own computers, but in 1950 few 13-year-olds owned typewriters. She often wondered:

> Why did he give it to me? I don't know. It may have been simply because he was sick of me sneaking into his office and using his typewriter—maybe he was nervous about the damage I might inflict as I endlessly, noisily taught myself how to type. But I like to think that he gave it to me because he recognized who I was, and what my dreams were, for the future.[18]

NEW SCHOOLS

Lois's family returned to Pennsylvania, where she entered her freshman year of high school. Again, though, the family did not stay settled. The next year they were in New York and living on Governors Island, an army base in New York Harbor. Because there were no high schools on the island, she enrolled at Curtis High School on Staten Island. It was not a pleasant experience. After the security of small-town Pennsylvania and the insular military community in Japan, the large public school was overwhelming. By the end of the year, she convinced her parents to let her transfer. She began to attend Packer Collegiate Institute, a private girls school in Brooklyn, in her junior year. In 1954, she graduated. She was only a few months past her seventeenth birthday.

Her parents wanted her to attend a state university in Pennsylvania where she would have qualified for low in-state tuition, but Lois was not interested. She settled the money issue by earning a scholarship to Brown University in Providence, Rhode Island.

She entered Brown in the fall of 1954, and she hoped to major in creative writing. Lois was certain that this was the first step in a smooth path toward becoming a successful writer. Instead, two years later, the simple gesture of a man she did not even remember helped change her life.

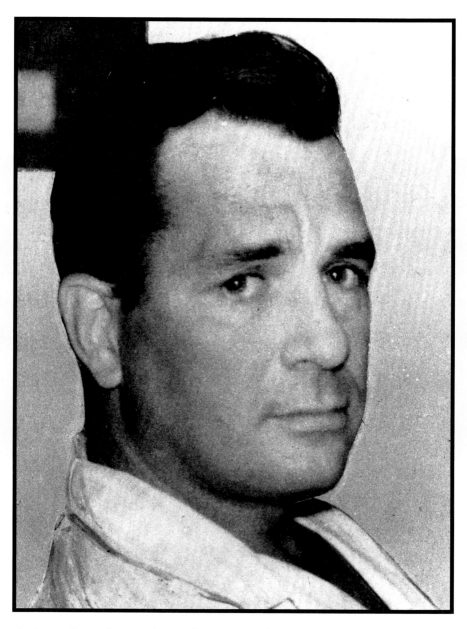

A photo of American author Jack Kerouac taken in 1962. Kerouac's energetic stream-of-consciousness novels, mostly notably On the Road, *inspired a generation of Americans to head out on the road to find themselves. Lois's own travels began about the same time, when she moved to California after marrying navy ensign Donald Grey Lowry.*

3

Western Gravity

I shambled after as I've been doing all my life after people who interest me, because the only people for me are the mad ones, the ones who are mad to live, mad to talk, mad to be saved, desirous of everything at the same time, the ones who never yawn or say a commonplace thing, but burn, burn, burn like fabulous yellow roman candles exploding like spiders across the stars and in the middle you see the blue centerlight pop and everybody goes "Awww!"[1]

—Jack Kerouac

Published in 1957, Jack Kerouac's *On the Road* depicts a group of rebellious and restless friends. In the novel, Kerouac stand-in Sal Paradise embarks on a series of road-trip escapades, and, like Paradise, the novel's other characters were based on real people. *On the Road* was the type of novel that attempts to capture a generation's dreams and their fears in a few hundred pages.

In 1920, F. Scott Fitzgerald's *This Side of Paradise* described the mood of young people just after World War I. Norman Mailer's *The Naked and the Dead* did the same thing after World War II. More recently, works such as Douglas Coupland's *Generation X: Tales for an Accelerated Culture* tell the stories of young people rebelling against society's expectations.

Fueled by gallons of coffee, Kerouac wrote *On the Road* in just a few weeks. Its stream-of-consciousness writing style was both praised for its immediacy and criticized by authors like Truman Capote, who famously quipped that the book was not writing but typing. The lifestyle it portrayed, though, based on the author's seven years of restless wandering, appealed to many young people who wanted to abandon the familiar in a quest for the unknown.

BROWN UNIVERSITY

Lois Lowry's own westward quest occurred a year before *On the Road* was published. Lois entered Brown University in Providence, Rhode Island, in 1954. Founded in 1764, this Ivy League university (one of the group of highly selective schools in the northeastern United States) has a long tradition of liberal curriculum requirements. In 1850, the school's president, Francis Wayland, wrote, "The various courses should be arranged, that, insofar as practicable, every student might study what he chose, all that he chose and nothing but what he chose."[2]

An aerial view of Brown University in Providence, Rhode Island. Lois dropped out of the university to marry Donald Lowry. She would not complete her bachelor's degree until 1973, two decades after leaving Brown.

Brown stood out in the conservative 1950s, and Lois was not completely prepared for college life. She was younger than her peers and a bit immature. She knew that she wanted to be a writer but was not certain of much else.

In her first year at Brown, from 1954 to 1955, Lois was "living in a very small dormitory, actually a converted private home, with a group of perhaps fourteen other girls. We are very much alike: we wear the same sort of clothes: cashmere sweaters and plaid wool skirts, knee socks and loafers."[3]

By her sophomore year, she was miserable and uncertain. She scribbled in notebooks and discussed politics in local coffeehouses. She slept through classes and wore a dirty army/navy store trench coat everywhere she went. She thought that she was finally rebelling by being different—except she was like many other young people she knew: angry and confused, with no idea what to do with the rest of their lives. Then an event changed her life.

In 1941, Edward MacFunn Biddle III had listened to a child recite a difficult poem. He was moved enough by Lois's reading of *Thanatopsis* to include her in his will. After he died, he left half of one percent of his estate to her. Because he was a wealthy man, it was a nice sum.

Perhaps Biddle envisioned amazing things for a girl he saw as a prodigy—a child gifted with a talent for language far beyond her years. Maybe he imagined that she would use the money to further her education or perhaps to spend a semester abroad.

Instead, Lois bought a car.

A NEW JOURNEY

In June 1956, Lois dropped out of school. She filled up her pale blue 1951 Pontiac with gas and everything she thought she would need (especially her typewriter) and "headed west into the sunset, to Southern California," she remembered in a speech. "My summons had come to join the innumerable caravan which moves to the mysterious realm."[4]

Many novels in addition to *On the Road* portray the main character's adventure when he or she leaves the familiar for a risky journey down unfamiliar roads. Lowry's most successful novel, *The Giver,* concludes with the main character riding his bike away from his village and

Did you know...

The series of books about Anastasia Krupnik's younger brother, Sam, was created because so many of Lowry's fans asked her for books about him. At first she was not sure how to tell a story from a baby's perspective, and when she handed in her manuscript, her editor was not sure that it would find an audience. It did, and today there are four books in the series.

coping with the challenges of the open road. Her light-hearted *See You Around, Sam* tells of a boy's attempt to run away to Alaska. It is a place where he believes people will understand him. At the very least, it is a place he imagines they will let him wear his plastic vampire fangs indoors.

Discussing this novel, Lowry said that "in every book—in order for there to be a book, a story, a point, a reason for writing it—the main character makes a journey."[5] So it was with Lois Lowry's story. Her adult life changed with a road trip, but it did not happen the same way it does in novels. Her life was altered before she packed her typewriter.

Lois had fallen in love. Donald Grey Lowry was a fellow student and a military officer. After a brief engagement, they were married. When Lois Lowry got in her car, it was to drive with her new husband to a San Diego naval base, where he would serve as a navy ensign.

"It was kind of a romanticized thing to do, but I . . . regret having dropped out of college," Lowry admits, "because it was one of those things women so often did in the fifties and that generation, was to relegate themselves to be handmaidens to husbands. I don't blame the husbands for that, but that's the role so many of us took. So many of us dropped out of college and gave up our own aspirations when we married as I did."[6]

Shortly before leaving Brown University, Lowry sat down with her writing professor, Charles Philbrick. He had read her work and was impressed with her talent. He had even given her an A in his course and told her, as she later recalled, "that I was a good writer. But he said, a little hesitantly, that I hadn't experienced very much yet. 'You need to suffer a grief,' he told me."[7]

It was prophecy. In a few years, she would suffer a heartbreaking loss that would inspire her first novel.

A photo of Lois Lowry and her four children in 1966. While she loved being a mother, Lowry found that it left her with little time to complete her degree and pursue a writing career.

4

Delayed Ambition

"I HAD ALWAYS wanted to be a writer, it's what I majored in in college," Lois Lowry explains, with the hindsight of knowing that her sudden marriage would interrupt her writing for nearly 20 years. Still, the sacrifice was also beneficial. "I think what I really needed to experience was life. You don't become a writer of any depth when you are seventeen, eighteen years old."

Besides, she admits, "If I had stayed in college and gone the conventional route I perhaps would not have ever had the career that I then later had. I probably would have gotten a job in publishing or whatever or maybe been an English professor. So again, it's probably a trade-off."[1]

Donald Grey Lowry was a military officer, just like Lois Lowry's father. The couple married when she was 19. For a few years, they settled into a routine of never staying in one place, and Lowry probably felt as if she was repeating her mother's life. Even if she figured out a way back to college, those ambitions faded with her first pregnancy—as did any immediate thoughts of a writing career.

After living in California, the couple moved to Connecticut, where their first child, a daughter named Alix, was born in 1958. From there, they moved to in Florida, where Lois had a son, Donald Grey Lowry Jr., but soon called Grey to differentiate him from his father. After that, it was South Carolina. With her children in diapers or learning to walk, there was little time for Lowry to write. Nearly as challenging, her husband left the military in 1960 to study at Harvard Law School in Cambridge, Massachusetts.

When Donald Grey began his studies, Lowry was a young mother of two. Considered one of the best law schools in the country, Harvard was also enormously demanding. The family was able to finally settle down for a few years, however, and while her husband studied, Lowry did all she could to help out. In addition to caring for the children, she typed manuscripts and worked part-time at the Harvard Co-op.

Their third child, Kristin, was born in 1961. Lowry loved being a mother, but she desperately wanted to go back to school. Perhaps she could take it slow, she thought, a course at a time, and signed up for a Russian language course at Harvard. She never completed the assignments. "I had been a good student in college, but I remember that I just couldn't find the time to do the studying that it required and it was so demoralizing to be doing poorly in an academic course."[2]

In 1962, she took a course closer to her heart: creative writing. Lowry couldn't write, however: She just didn't have time. "I loved the class," Lowry remembers, "it met once a week and I looked forward to that Wednesday night so much, but I never found the time to get the assignments done."[3] She was in her final trimester with her fourth child when she began the course. In mid-November, she missed a class to give birth to the couple's last child, Benjamin.

Somehow, she managed to return to class the very next week. Eyeing the suddenly slimmer Lowry, the professor commented, "I'm glad to see you've done something creative this semester."[4] The casual criticism cut Lowry to the quick.

TRAGEDY STRIKES

A few months before, while pregnant with Benjamin, Lois Lowry had learned the sad news that her sister, Helen, had been diagnosed with cancer. Professor Charles Philbrick's "wish" that she suffer a tragedy to sharpen her talent had come true.

Helen spent her last weeks in a Washington, D.C. hospital. Although Lowry wanted badly to visit, her parents convinced her not to go. Exposing her unborn child to the germs in the hospital was too great a risk. There would be plenty of time to see Helen when she got out of the hospital.

She never did. Lowry remembered standing outside a funeral home with her brother:

> Our sister's body lay inside. Jon was in college and I was a college drop-out, a young wife and a new mother. We had been summoned to Pennsylvania by her death. We were young, and sad, and uncertain. . . . We were probably both frightened by the sudden awareness of how tenuous everything was: how easily it could slip away. . . . It was as if the raised cracks in the

A photo of the Hammersberg sisters, Helen (left) at 18 and Lois at 15. The death of Lois's sister in 1962 would profoundly impact her life and her writing.

sidewalk, the places we had learned to roller-skate over, had suddenly shifted and heaved again, without warning and now we had to look at what had been thrust upward and dislodged, had to learn how to find our footing again.[5]

It would take time for Lois Lowry to find her footing as a writer.

A NEW HOME

After Lowry's husband graduated from law school in 1963, he accepted a position in Portland, Maine. Lowry recalled in her photo memoir, *Looking Back: A Book of Memories*:

> Because my family moved so often during my childhood, we always seemed to be saying goodbye to things: dogs went to new homes, books were packed away in boxes and donated to libraries. As a parent, I think I tried, in a way, to create for my children the kind of life I yearned for as a child myself: a house that was always ours, books that were there to be read again and again, and pets that followed you home and were allowed to stay.[6]

Unable to find time to write, Lowry told stories to her children. Having a captive—but occasionally critical audience—was good training for a future children's author.

BACK TO SCHOOL

In the late 1960s, Lowry's youngest child started kindergarten and Lowry returned to school. At 31, she was considerably older than most of her classmates at the University of Southern Maine (USM). "By the time I went back to college in my thirties, my father gave me an electric portable typewriter," she remembers. "Even though it's romantic to think I was plugging away on a manual typewriter, it had actually been upgraded."[7] Unable to attend full-time, Lowry took four years to complete two years of course work. She earned her bachelor's degree in 1973, two decades after matriculating at Brown.

Novelists often start their writing careers in nonfiction. The reason is simple: There are more markets for nonfiction—a greater number of places to be published. Almost every town, no matter how small, has its own newspaper. More magazines publish articles than short stories, and publishers produce more nonfiction books than novels.

Encouraged by her professors, Lowry began to write articles for small newspapers and magazines on a freelance basis. When a USM professor planned a series of short textbooks, he hired Lowry to write two of them, *Literature of the American Revolution* and *Black American Literature*. She went to graduate school and even studied photography. Taking the pictures that accompanied the articles she wrote improved her marketability.

Attending Bread Loaf School of English, a prestigious writers' workshop in Middlebury, Vermont, also sharpened her craft. By now she was writing more than she ever had

Did you know...

The Bread Loaf School of English near Middlebury, Vermont, began as an inn but was willed to Middlebury College in 1915. Since then, it has educated hundreds of graduate students and hosted numerous guest instructors for its six weeks of instruction in creative writing, English, theater, and literature. Poet Robert Frost taught there for nearly 40 years.

as an adult. Still, family life consumed most of her time. She was not able to focus on a novel; short stories of 15 to 20 pages each were all she managed. "I suppose really I didn't have the extended time because I was so interrupted by family commitments and by the needs of four kids that short stories were all I could manage at that time," the author admits.[8]

A good imagination is inside the toolbox every writer carries, but sometimes they imagine the worst. Lowry worried that a house fire might torch her stories. To protect them, she stored pages in the vegetable crisper of her refrigerator. Later, Anastasia Krupnik's father used the same technique in one of Lowry's novels.

NEW TROUBLES

As her writing improved, Lowry's marriage faltered. Growing up in the 1950s, young women were taught that their most important job was taking care of their husbands and children; everything else was a hobby. Lowry earned her degree and a paycheck from writing, but to her husband, she might as well have been knitting.

Donald Lowry kept a study at their house so that he could work on evenings and weekends. When his wife began to write, she did not disturb his desk. Instead, she set up a card table in a corner of the room, furnishing it with pens, paper, and a typewriter. "I came home and my typewriter was missing and I thought it had been stolen," the author remembers.

> I was very upset and I called my husband and he said, "No, no," he had loaned it to someone working as a volunteer on a political campaign. So, his motives were not malevolent, I'll give him that, but what it meant was that he really had no understanding of me, of how important it was to me—I had a

connection to that machine that he didn't appreciate. . . . I do remember it as a black moment.[9]

WHAT TO WRITE?

Although she had been paid to write articles, this was not the kind of writing she wanted to do. Lowry sent her short stories to magazines, hoping to see one published—but it was a long shot. "What I really wanted to do was write fiction and I was writing short stories and at the same time that I was selling a good bit of nonfiction, journalistic stuff, I was trying to sell short fiction and I wasn't succeeding."[10]

When Lowry was a child, dozens of popular magazines published short fiction. Every decade, fewer and fewer did. By the 1970s, the competition to publish a short story was fierce. For years, Lowry got one rejection letter after another—but they did not stop her.

Lowry told an audience at Brown University:

In 1975—age 38, in case you haven't been counting, I woke up one fall morning and the smell in the air, a smell of dry leaves and late apples—reminded me of a day twenty-nine years before. My father, newly home from the war, had taken me—just me, not my sister or my brother—on an outing. We were new and unfamiliar to each other, and we were tentative with our affection.[11]

"Crow Call," the short story that developed from her recollection, was Lowry's first success at selling her fiction. Published in *Redbook*, a popular magazine for women, the story was written from the perspective of a nine-year-old girl. Lowry did not realize that what she had written was similar to short stories written for young adults. What she knew of the category stretched back to reading *The Yearling* as a kid herself. Once Lowry stopped reading to her children, she stopped reading books that were not written for adults.

Publishing a short story, however, while difficult, is not as daunting a task as getting a novel published. Every year creative writing programs, like the ones at the University of Iowa and the University of California at Irvine, produce graduates with novels and connections. More novels are crafted in seminars, workshops, extension courses, library carrels, coffee shops, and writers' homes and offices.

These manuscripts are sent by the thousands to major New York publishers like Random House, Viking, and Doubleday, as well as smaller publishing houses. They are often unsolicited and are dumped into the "slush pile." Eventually, they are skimmed by unpaid interns, who rarely pass them on to editors and instead return them to their authors with a form rejection letter.

A SPECIAL REQUEST

Many writers are seeking publishers, but, occasionally, a publisher seeks out a writer. That is what happened to Lois Lowry when she got a letter forwarded from her editor at *Redbook*. It came with a note: "I remember the magazine editor saying enclosed is a letter from an enterprising editor," Lowry remembered.[12]

Melanie Kroupa was an editor at Houghton Mifflin, a major publisher. She was impressed by the story and advised Lowry, "You should be writing for kids."[13] Would Lowry consider writing a novel for young adults?

Lowry explained:

I had seen myself, or hoped to be able to see myself, as a writer for adults. When she invited me to write a novel for young adults, for her publishing company, I took it on as a project because it was so unusual to be asked to write something. They didn't promise to publish it, but the fact that they took an interest in me and would give it careful attention, was encouraging, so I then sat down and drew on the experience I'd had of losing my sister.[14]

Although Helen was in her 20s when she died, the characters in the book were teenagers. In it, Lowry incorporated many of their experiences growing up—including the fact that Helen really drew a line down the middle of their shared room because she thought Lois was a slob.

Pain is not diminished because an artist can paint or write poetry or craft a book for teenagers—not in the beginning. Time does not heal all wounds, but it can allow a writer to turn heartache into literature.

The narrator in one of Lowry's later novels, *Autumn Street*, describes the process:

> What is true is this: by the time you realize how much something mattered, time has passed; by the time it stops hurting enough that you can tell about it, first to yourself and finally to someone else, more time has passed, then when you sit down to begin the telling, you have to begin this way: It was a long time ago.[15]

THE FIRST NOVEL

Lois Lowry wrote her first novel, *A Summer to Die*, more than a dozen years after Helen's funeral. By then, she had emotional distance from the tragedy. Like all fiction writers who use life experiences in their work, Lowry changed details; it was not a memoir after all. In her novel, the 13-year-old main character, Meg, is forced to share a room with Molly, her older sister, after their family moves to Pennsylvania. The move at the novel's opening mirrors

Lowry's move to the same state at the beginning of World War II. Lowry also gave Meg many of her own qualities: somewhat quiet and introspective, more an observer than participant. Molly, like Helen, was a vivacious blonde, a little boy-crazy, and concerned with her appearance.

Growing up, Lowry found comfort in writing; for Meg it was photography. Little Lois's grandfather encouraged her to read; Meg's 70-year-old neighbor encourages her to take pictures.

Meg says in the book that "After a while, you remember the good things more often than the bad."[16] In her afterword to the novel, Lowry agreed:

> I remember Helen giggling. I remember the two of us fighting over who was taking up too much room in the back seat. How we borrowed each other's clothes (and even once dated the same boy). Somehow, magically, mercifully, I no longer remember her ill. That's because mostly what is real is the way life continues, and the way people become able to absorb loss, to value memories and to say goodbye.[17]

THE END

As she was working on her novel, Lowry's marriage was ending. In 1977, the couple separated. Lowry's youngest child remained with his father so that he would not have to switch schools. Lowry had moved enough as a teenager to know how hard that could be.

Her pending divorce was not the only challenge Lowry faced. While she was writing her first novel, Melanie Kroupa left Houghton Mifflin. The woman who discovered Lowry was no longer her champion. The aspiring author would have to take a chance with an unfamiliar editor who did not know her and did not know her work.

Stephen King, an enormously popular American writer best known for his horror fiction, has been Lowry's good friend since 1977. That summer King asked her to review the manuscript to his novel The Dead Zone, *which was published in 1979 and has since been adapted into a film and a television series.*

5

Second Beginnings

EARLY SUCCESSES

Susan Eloise Hinton kept getting Ds in her creative writing class. The junior at Will Rogers High School in Tulsa, Oklahoma, had begun a novel the year before. Now she wondered if she could ever be a "real writer." After all, her teacher didn't think so. Eventually she told one of her friends about the book she had been working on, "and her mother happened to write children's books. I gave her a copy of *The Outsiders*, and this woman showed it to a friend who had a New York agent. The agent liked it, and sold it to the second publisher who read it.

She has been my agent ever since. I received the contract from the publisher on graduation day!"[1]

Because it was written from a boy's point of view, her publisher encouraged the author to go by her initials. S.E. Hinton's *The Outsiders* describes an increasingly violent rivalry between the affluent "Socs" and the poorer "Greasers." Since its publication in 1967, the novel has sold more than 8 million copies. In 1983, it was turned into a movie and featured some of the earliest performances of future movie stars such as Tom Cruise, Matt Dillon, and Patrick Swayze.

Christopher Paolini's *Eragon* began as a self-published novel—its printings paid for by the author's family. The fantasy dragon story attracted young readers in droves, and they often bought the book after attending one of the 135 readings the author staged in bookshops, libraries, and schools. When the book was published by Knopf in 2003 and optioned by 20th Century Fox's Fox 2000 Pictures, the home-schooled author was still in his teens.

Few authors publish their debut novels as teenagers, but many sign their first book contracts in their twenties. Charles Dickens was a 24–year-old reporter when *The Pickwick Papers* went from being a serialized column to a book in 1836. F. Scott Fitzgerald was a 22-year-old college dropout living with his parents in Minnesota when *This Side of Paradise* was bought by Scribner's. At 26, Stephen King was teaching high school English and working summers at an industrial laundry when *Carrie* was sold first to Doubleday and then had its paperback rights auctioned to Signet Books for $400,000.

"I met Steve [King] in 1977 . . . a magazine sent me to do an article on him and we became friends," Lowry explains.[2] Not far from where King was launching his career as an author, Lois Lowry was 40 and wondering if anyone would read her first novel.

DEDICATION

Like many successful writers, Lowry cautions that fame and fortune should not be the reason one writes. "Very, very few writers become rich and famous," Lowry tells aspiring writers on her Web site. "*Stephen King and J. K. Rowling. They are very unusual. Most writers don't even make a living by writing. If you want to become rich, then you should invent something like EBAY; or maybe be an orthodontist; but writing won't do it.*"[3]

"I would be a writer, if I only had the time," complains nearly everyone with an idea who believes that, with a spare

Did you know...

It is nice to be a published novelist at 15, but as writer Ariel Gore points out, unlike many careers, being a novelist means it is never too late: "James Michener was forty when he published *Tales of the South Pacific.* Frank McCourt was a sixty-six-year-old retired schoolteacher when *Angela's Ashes* came out. Maya Angelou published her debut memoir, *I Know Why the Caged Bird Sings,* at forty-two. Fannie Flagg was forty-three when *Fried Green Tomatoes at the Whistle Stop Cafe* came out."[*]

* Ariel Gore, *How to Become a Famous Writer Before You're Dead: Your Words in Print and Your Name in Lights.* New York: Crown, 2007, p. 29.

moment or two, his or her idea would magically become a novel. Plumbers and engineers are rarely approached by people who confide how much they dream of someday repairing their own pipes or erecting a bridge, yet published authors quickly learn that nearly all people believe that they have a story in them. . . . If only they had the time.

"But I don't have any time to write," author and teacher Ariel Gore recalls one student's complaint. "And I don't ask her how it is, then, that she has time to come to class. I'm glad to have her, even empty-handed. Instead I offer some suggestions: If you don't have time to write, stop answering the phone. Change your e-mail address. Kill your television."[4]

Lois Lowry was a mother facing divorce, but she had made the time to finish her novel. She submitted it to Walter Lorraine, a different editor from the one who had encouraged her to write for young adults. Lowry endured some nervous moments while she waited for his response.

Lorraine had been an editor for decades. The dark themes in Lowry's first book were unusual, but he loved it. In 1976, Houghton Mifflin accepted the book. Lowry was given a small advance—money given to an author before a book's publication based on sales. Although it was not enough money to change her life, it did help her with changes she was planning to make even before she signed a publishing contract.

ON HER OWN

Marriages end for different reasons. By the time Lowry's first book was in bookstores, she had moved out of the family house in Maine. "I left the house where I had lived comfortably for many years. I took only my car, my typewriter and my clothes. Everything I owned fit into my Honda

Civic," Lowry later recalled in a speech. "When nothing is provided for you, you have to provide it for yourself, and so you become self-disciplined, and self-discipline is an awfully good thing for a writer to have."[5]

Despite her age, Lowry had never lived alone before. Today, she admits that not only did her children grow up in Maine, but she did in many ways as well. It was the place where she finally graduated from college and cashed her first paycheck as a writer. It was also where she hoped to carve out a living as a novelist.

In the summer of 1977, she moved into an unheated but furnished garage apartment. She did not need much, though. As she earned her living banging away on a typewriter, she must have felt a connection to the young girl she had once been, writing stories in her father's den.

A NEW BOOK

As *A Summer to Die* was being published, Lowry worked on her second novel. *Find a Stranger, Say Goodbye* focused on a young girl named Natalie and her quest to meet her birth mother. The book also portrayed the isolation that Natalie's birth mother felt as a pregnant teenager.

Lowry's first novel grew from her own experiences with her older sister, but her second came more from her imagination. Unlike Natalie, Lowry was not adopted and was a married adult when she had her first child. Still, being the "new kid" in so many schools left her achingly familiar with being a lonely outsider and had turned her into a talented observer.

In the 1970s, when *Find a Stranger, Say Goodbye* was written, most adoptions were "closed," and the adopted child did not have contact with his or her birth mother. Today, many adoptions are "open," meaning that the birth mother stays in contact with her child. In some cases, the birth mother occasionally visits the adoptive parents' home.

Second novels are challenging for writers. Even with the promise of a careful read by an editor, Lowry was alone when she worked on her first book. She did not feel as if anyone was looking over her shoulder. As she typed her second book, she had deadlines, a contract, and an editor. The attention may have made the writing process tougher. *Find a Stranger, Say Goodbye* was not considered as successful as her first. The sophomore slump, as it is sometimes called, afflicts many writers, and according to some of her more negative reviews, it cursed Lowry as well. "The author of *A Summer to Die*, a capable writer, is totally at ease with the topical novel; once again she is thoroughly au courant," the review from *The Horn Book Magazine* began. "But the attractiveness of the characters and the tidiness of the plot constitute the weakness of the book."[6]

FIRST SUCCESS

As she was finishing her second book, her first one was attracting readers. "I got my first fan letters—a few scraps from adolescent girls—as a result of that book," Lowry remembered, "but I had no way of knowing whether it would do well, sell well, or what 'doing well' meant."[7]

In 1978, Lowry won the International Reading Association's Children's Literature Award for *A Summer to Die*. She was excited but told Lorraine that she would not be able to go to Houston to attend the awards ceremony. He asked her why. She told him that she could not afford the airfare. Lowry's editor laughed. The award was prestigious and would give the author's first novel attention and help it sell. The publishing company would pay the expenses.

Two thousand people attended the ceremony. Lowry was worried. "Do I have to make a speech?" she asked her editor. His face fell. She didn't have a speech ready?

"I didn't," she admitted later. "But I made one anyway, because everyone was looking at me and I had to say something; and so I told them that the population of the room was four times larger than the population of my town; and that the check they gave me for one thousand dollars was four times larger than the amount of money I had made the previous month."[8]

The next month, she spoke at a local eighth grade graduation and her life's focus sharpened. Before that graduation, she had been a writer who happened to write for young adults. She realized the impact of her words on young people at that ceremony and from the dozens of letters her editor sent her from readers across the country (and soon all over the world) who were touched by her novels about loss and adoption. Lowry realized, "And only then, for the first time, did I perceive that when I, as a child, sought from stories something that I had no name for, it had simply been, unquestioning intimacy I needed. A place to listen with one's heart. Glimpsed light spilling from a warm kitchen into the dark staircase where I sat alone."[9]

Lois Lowry is an in-demand speaker. In her speeches, she often describes her life experiences, including her years-long struggle to make a name for herself as an author.

6

Bright Paths

EARNINGS FROM AWARDS and novels were not making Lois Lowry rich, and money remained a struggle:

I found another place to live—someone's guest house—it wasn't furnished. So I bought parts of a bed from a second-hand store, and I borrowed wicker porch furniture from a friend, and my ex-husband's new wife gave me my old pine kitchen table because it had been my grandmother's, and I bought a painting, a landscape done by a painter friend which cost three hundred dollars. Nobody could understand why someone who didn't own a television or a whole set of dishes would buy a painting.[1]

As fall deepened into winter, she struggled with her third novel. Lowry explained at a 1997 Children's Literature New England (CLNE) lecture:

> Most of what I do as a writer I do by subconscious and whim and intuition. It is only in the looking back that I can see patterns to what I have done, the way we sometimes take pleasure in reading a road map after a trip has come to an end: seeing where we turned, remembering why, and recalling with sighs or smiles the outcomes of shortcuts or detours.[2]

A PERSONAL WORK

Autumn Street was nearly a memoir. It was fiction, but it featured clear details from the author's childhood experiences in Pennsylvania during World War II. In *A Summer to Die* she based the older sister on Helen but made the character more than a decade younger when she died of cancer. The sisters in *Autumn Street* were the same age as the Lowry sisters had been. Like Lois, young Elizabeth copes not only with an absent father and an unfamiliar town but also with her mother's focus on a new baby and her sister's focus on her new friends:

> I remembered, suddenly, the little girl I was once, lonely in my stern grandmother's house, warmed and welcomed only in the kitchen, by the black woman—who had a name but was called only "the cook"—and whom I had last seen at my sister's funeral, as she stood apart and alone at the cemetery. Her own grandchild had been murdered years before, and now, thinking of it, I realized I did not even know where that child was buried.[3]

Fleta Jordan's granddaughter had been young Lois's closest friend. Lowry changed the gender and had the murder occur shortly before Elizabeth's injured father returns from the war. Lowry retained many other elements from the time, including the separations created by class and race and the prejudice endured by Jordan and other African Americans in the 1940s.

It was a dark and powerful novel, but Lowry abruptly set it aside. She needed some lightness and joy in her life, which came in the form of a new character, Anastasia Krupnik. "It was winter in Maine," she recalled, "snowy, icy, cold. I was poor and I chose to make myself laugh."[4] In Maine during the winter, first snow often arrives in October; the last big storm frequently hits in April. During those six months, when it isn't snowing, the sky is often gray and the sun sets before five. Even on clear sunny days, the blowing wind can make it feel like 20 degrees below zero. In that environment, Lowry was alone and living in a small guesthouse.

THE BEGINNING OF A SERIES

"Anastasia Krupnik was ten," the novel opens. "She had hair the color of Hubbard squash, fourteen freckles across her nose (and seven others in places that she preferred people not to know about) and glasses with owl-eyed rims, which she had chosen herself at the opticians."[5]

Like Lowry did as a girl, Anastasia keeps her "loves" and "hates" listed in a notebook. Nearly every day the list changes: Her "loves" become "hates" or vice versa. Through most of the book, the pending arrival of her baby brother consistently earns a spot on the hate list. When Anastasia's parents decide that she should name him when he is born, she secretly records a name so vulgar that today Lowry doubts a publisher would allow it in a book for elementary school children. Lowry admits:

> That astonishes me looking back on it. If I were to try to do that today, I would not be able to, it wouldn't be published. The editor would make me take it out because there's been a very substantial move toward more censorship of children's books, sanctioned by our conservative government in recent years, so publishers are much more careful.[6]

Did you know...

The American Library Association (ALA) keeps a list of "challenged books." A book is challenged when a formal request is made to remove it from a school library (usually by a parent). The ALA records it. Usually the book remains on shelves. Occasionally, the book is pulled, often by the school board. Lois Lowry has regularly been in the top-10-most-challenged authors, most recently in 2005. *The Giver* has been challenged regularly, but so have many of her lighter novels, including her early Anastasia Krupnik books.

While Kennebunkport is best known as the vacation home of the forty-first U.S. president, George H.W. Bush, it is also the subject of one of Lois Lowry's early nonfiction works, a guidebook titled Here in Kennebunkport, *for which she took the photos.*

A SHARPER FOCUS

As the decade ended, so too did Lowry's work in nonfiction. Her photographs of a scenic town in coastal Maine popular with tourists and famous now as the summer home of former president George Herbert Walker Bush appeared in a guidebook, *Here in Kennebunkport*. She took the assignment for one reason: She needed the money.

By 1980, she had three published novels that were serious literary works and another, *Anastasia Krupnik*, which was not only humorous but would spawn an entire series. Lowry quickly realized that fan letters and connections do not just come from books with darker themes. One fan, Paula from Louisville, Kentucky, wrote to Lowry:

> I really like the book you wrote about Anastasia and her family because it made me laugh every time I read it. I especially liked when it said she didn't want to have a baby brother in the house because she had to clean up after him every time and change his diaper when her mother and father aren't home and she doesn't like to give him a bath and watch him all the time and put him to sleep every night while her mother goes to work.

"Here's the fascinating thing," Lowry offered a 1994 audience. "Nothing that the child describes actually happens in the book. The child—as we all do—has brought her own life to a book. She has found a place, a place in

Did you know...

In 2008, Kennebunkport was featured on a Home and Garden Television special, "Top Ten Christmas Towns." The program showcased the unique holiday traditions of the port town.

the pages of a book, that shares her own frustration and feelings."[7]

The 1980s would find the author developing multiple series and authoring numerous literary novels for a young adult audience. It would also be a time when she would consider the raw power of the books she and others wrote for kids growing up in the later part of the twentieth century.

Above, Lois Lowry (center) *at a book signing. Lowry's popularity as an author increased considerably after being awarded the Newbery Medal twice: first for* Number the Stars *in 1990, and again for* The Giver *in 1994.*

7

Hidden Powers

WHEN LOIS LOWRY's mother was dying, she would lie in bed and tell stories to her daughter. Although blind, Katherine Hammersberg could still see into her past. She told Lois about her life as a young girl in the early 1900s. Lowry had heard these recollections before, but growing up she did not pay much attention. Now she listened.

One story stood out. Her mother happily talked about her best friend, a little girl who lived next door—next door to the same Pennsylvania house Lowry stayed in during World War II. Midway through telling the story, however, Hammersberg's face darkened as she described the girl's father and her siblings.

Repeating her mother's words, Lowry told an audience at Brown University:

> He beat them. We could hear them yelling. My mother would close the windows on that side of the house.
>
> "Isn't that odd?" she said. "That we never said anything? I suppose today it would be called child abuse."
>
> I agreed with her that it was odd, and sad, and startling. Privately I was thinking: that quiet street. *Those large, lovely houses.* All of those closed windows. . . . *So much for the sanctity of my idyllic childhood.* My town—its bright streets truly a treacherous memory—was filled with very dark paths.[1]

YOUNG ADULT FICTION—A SERIOUS SIDE

Nostalgia often convinces people that life was once easier, yet the pain endured by children like Hammersberg's best friend was as common then as it is today. The difference is that such suffering was once hidden and there was rarely the sense it even existed in the books written for young people at the time.

In the same speech, Lowry quoted her friend, a child psychologist:

> "There is only one thing worse than feeling hopeless, helpless and worthless. And that is feeling hopeless, helpless, worthless and *alone.*"
>
> My mother's little friend, whipped each night by her father, went out each morning and was greeted by neighbors—including my own grandmother—who had closed the windows against the sound. How alone that child must have felt. How helpless.
>
> But what would her books have been? Elsie Dinsmore? Rebecca of Sunnybrook Farm? There was no resource or comfort in the young people's fiction of that time.[2]

In order for there to be books for young adults, realistic or otherwise, there have to be young adults. For centuries, however, the years between childhood's end and adulthood were not acknowledged as a different phase of life. Throughout most of the 1800s, the United States was an agrarian society, based on farming. Children of farmers worked for their families from a young age, and education was viewed as an interruption not a necessity. The "summer break" between grades, still common today, began because children labored on family farms during the summer.

Few of these children went to school past their early teens. At 15 or 16, many were starting families of their own. In the cities, children's lives were even grimmer—many spent 12 hours or more every day working at factories.

In the early 1900s, laws that prohibited children from dangerous factory work and fewer farms reduced the need for young labor. At the same time, society required a more educated populace, and every year more teenagers graduated from high school. A period of time between childhood and adulthood was acknowledged, but literature for young adults evolved more slowly.

Lowry remembers the books her mother read to her as a young girl, like Frances Hodgson Burnett's *The Secret Garden* and Marjorie Kinnan Rawlings's *The Yearling*, a Pulitzer Prize-winning novel that is still popular decades after its publication in 1938. The work dealt with loss, a recurrent theme in Lowry's novels.

There were few books for young people that dealt with darker themes. Well into the 1950s, books such as the Nancy Drew and Hardy Boys series were marketed to teens decades after their first appearance. In the first half of the twentieth century, books for young adults had one thing in common: Readers were not supposed to come away just entertained, they were supposed to learn an important value such as thrift or chastity. By the 1960s, however, the social changes that affected other areas of culture such as movies, music, and television began to affect young adult literature as well.

"One of my reasons for writing [*The Outsiders*] was that I wanted something realistic to be written about teenagers," author S.E. Hinton explained in the afterword to her novel. "At that time, realistic teen fiction didn't exist. If you didn't want to read *Mary Jane Goes to the Prom* and you were through with horse books, there was nothing to read."[3]

When S.E. Hinton's *The Outsiders* was published by Viking Press in 1967, it was an enormously popular young adult novel, selling more than 8 million copies. In 1975, Judy Blume's *Forever* broke more boundaries by dealing with teenage sex and the fear of with teen pregnancy. By the

Did you know...

Lowry's grandmother read *The Secret Garden*, a children's novel by Frances Hodgson Burnett, to her daughter, who read it to Lowry, who read it to her daughter and her granddaughter. Published in 1911, the book has spawned various sequels and films based on the original story.

time Blume's work was becoming popular, Lowry's early novels that dealt with controversial subjects were finding an audience.

Young adult fiction is categorized by having an adolescent protagonist, or main character. Many modern young adult novels feature 17-year-old protagonists because writers and publishers believe that readers younger than 17 enjoy reading books featuring characters who are almost adults. Books with characters in their early teens are believed to be less interesting to older teens. Although most of Lowry's books feature slightly younger main characters—between the ages of 10 and 14—her books often appeal to older readers. In fact, Lowry's audience ranges from elementary school students to adults. Her trilogy that began with *The Giver* and includes *Gathering Blue* and *Messenger* has been republished with different covers and located in the adult literature sections of bookstores, alongside works by authors like Elmore Leonard and Cormac McCarthy.

GENRES

Like adult novels, young adult books are categorized by genre, such as mystery, science fiction, or romance. Series such as *Gossip Girl*, *Sisterhood of the Traveling Pants*, and *The Insiders* attract their own loyal audiences. Some series are actually produced by multiple authors laboring under the same pseudonym like Carolyn Keene's Nancy Drew books.

Books that are categorized as literary fiction feature well-developed characters, poetic descriptions, and realistic, if occasionally unfamiliar, settings. Adult works often earn awards like the National Book Award or the Pulitzer Prize. Some, like the ones featured on Oprah's Book Club, are frequently both literary *and* bestsellers. Most literary works, however, appeal to a smaller audience than genre novels do.

"If you happen to be a science fiction fan, it's natural that you should want to write science fiction," Stephen King explained in his book *On Writing*. "If you're a mystery fan, you'll want to write mysteries and if you enjoy romances, it's natural for you to want to write romances of your own. There's nothing wrong with any of those things."[4]

Lowry did not follow King's formula precisely: She does not read novels written for children or teenagers. "No, I did not and I still do not, so I did not follow Steve's advice really," Lowry laughs. "My strength was using my own childhood, my memories were very clear to me and very vibrant. I've always had a capacity to remember things complete with their sounds and smells and colors and I drew on that and the fact that I liked kids."[5] In her private life, Lowry's favorite books are ones written for adults and categorized as literary fiction—like many of the books she writes for young people.

Lowry also avoided a common downfall with popular novels. "I try to avoid things like contemporary vernacular because those things get dated so quickly," she explains. By avoiding current slang or having characters reference new movies or television programs, the novels did not become dated. That's a big reason why many of the books she penned in the 1980s are still popular today.

Lowry avoids criticizing trendy novels, the ones that seem like they were written last month and go out of print as soon as the next generation of cell phones hits the stores. "Those who do that succeed in the short run because there is a lot of that stuff published," she concedes, "it just doesn't stay around very long."[6] In the 1990s, Lowry would craft novels that would have an enduring legacy she could not have imagined.

Above, Nazi leader Adolf Hitler being saluted by his men. One of the most monstrous dictators the world has ever known, Hitler was the architect of the Holocaust—the genocide of 6 million European Jews during World War II. In Number the Stars, Lowry's novel about the Holocaust, a young girl is caught up in the rescue of Danish Jews.

8

Turning Away

IN GREEK MYTHOLOGY, Icarus did not listen to his father. Daedalus, his father, crafted wings from feathers and wax so that he and his son could escape from their exile in Crete. Just before their flight, the father gave Icarus a final warning: Do not fly too high or the heat of the sun will melt the wax. Icarus did not listen. Enjoying the freedom of flight, he soared ever higher. The wax melted and Icarus plunged to his death.

This myth was depicted in a 1558 painting, *Landscape with the Fall of Icarus*, by Pieter Brueghel the Elder. In a speech, Lois Lowry quoted W.H. Auden's poem, "Musée des Beaux

Arts," which describes the painting: "In Breughel's Icarus, for instance: how everything turns away quite leisurely from the disaster."[1] In the painting, the young boy is scarcely visible as he drowns, ignored by everyone.

When it was created, the painting was a comment on the reckless folly of youth. By the time Auden penned his poem in 1938, it reflected a darker theme. Confronted with tragedy, do witnesses get involved and take a risk? Do they try to change events? Or do they turn away?

IDEA FOR A NEW NOVEL

Sitting in a German prison, failed painter Adolf Hitler crafted a treatise that would lead to the death of millions. *Mein Kampf*, or *My Struggle*, outlined his belief in the superiority of those he called Aryan: fair-skinned, blue-eyed blond Germans—this despite the fact that Hitler himself was a dark-haired man. It was, he wrote, a Jewish conspiracy that kept the so-called master race from ascending to its natural place of ruling power.

Unlike most visions fueled by racism and fear, Hitler's came to fruition. After leaving prison following his failed 1923 uprising in Munich, Hitler moved rapidly to gain power in post–World War I Germany. Faced with huge debts imposed by the victorious forces led by Great Britain, France, and the United States, the economy in Germany was in freefall. Inflation spiraled out of control, and jobs were scarce. Preaching a message of a return of German pride, Hitler found an interested and growing audience.

The Nazi Party became the dominant party in the German parliament in 1932; in January 1933, Hitler became chancellor. Hitler turned his party's victory in democratic elections into an all-controlling government power—Germany became a dictatorship. His Nazi army enforced strict rules on all aspects of life, from what newspapers could print to what schools could teach.

As his army invaded countries like Poland and France, anti-Semitism, the belief that Jewish people are inferior, became the policy in the conquered countries. At first, Nazi policies restricted Jews' property rights and dictated where they could live. Increasingly authoritarian laws required Jews to register with the police, relocate to ghettos, and wear yellow stars on their clothing for identification. Eventually, hundreds of thousands boarded trains bound for concentration camps and execution.

In the years afterward, many wondered about the people who had been the friends, neighbors, and coworkers of the Jews. Why did so many of them turn away?

Lowry crafted a novel that depicted people who did not turn away. The idea grew from a friend's recollections. While Lowry was growing up in western Pennsylvania, her friend Annelise Platt was an elementary school girl in Copenhagen, Denmark. Their childhood experiences, however, were radically different. Lowry avoided a nervous grandmother; Platt avoided Nazis.

Adolf Hitler's Nazi army entered Denmark in 1940, and the country's king surrendered. He knew that his nation's small army was no match for the German war machine. When the Nazis took over, they ran the newspapers, the government, and the schools. They tried to commandeer the Danish navy but were thwarted by resistance fighters, who blew up the vessels to keep the Nazis from operating them. The Nazis also brought their anti-Semitic policies to Denmark. Throughout Europe, Jews in Nazi-occupied countries were being forced into concentration camps, where many were either worked to death or systematically executed. (By the time World War II ended, more than 6 million Jews—from the very young to the very old—had been murdered.)

That fate awaited Danish Jews as surely as it did the Jews of Holland, Poland, France, and elsewhere. Speaking to Platt, Lowry learned that the Danes did not allow the Nazis to take their Jewish friends and neighbors. Instead, they helped Jews evade capture and leave the country. Nearly the

Did you know...

The Web site for Barnes and Noble lists more than 6,700 items under the category of "Jewish Holocaust." *Anne Frank: The Diary of a Young Girl* is so widely read that it is the eighth-bestselling book in the category, partly because the tragic memoir still speaks to many. Jane Yolen's *The Devil's Arithmetic* is a very popular young adult book on the subject and was made into a movie starring Kirsten Dunst. Despite being written nearly 20 years ago, Lowry's *Number the Stars* is in the category's top 10. In 2008, the number-one book in the category is Elie Wiesel's *Night*, an autobiography about his experiences in Nazi concentration camps.

entire Jewish population of Denmark, about 7,000 people, was smuggled across the water to Sweden.

After listening to Platt's recollections, Lowry had an idea for a book unlike any she had written. "Although I enjoy writing lighthearted stories," she later said in an interview, "like the books about Anastasia, Sam and Gooney Bird Greene—I love knowing that I have also written books that can affect young people's lives. That knowledge keeps me at it."[2]

Number the Stars depicted Danish resistance from the perspective of Annemarie Johansen. The 10-year old girl's best friend, Ellen Rosen, is Jewish. Johansen's family risks death to help the Rosen family escape. The fictional experiences of one young girl connected readers to the plight of millions half a century earlier. Despite its setting in World War II, Lowry's novel was similar to her other stand-alone books because the main character was a young person facing both heart-wrenching loss and everyday confrontations with siblings and parents. The novel's drama was heightened by its unique historical setting.

The novel worried the author. With other books, her research focused on personal experiences with perhaps a quick trip to a nearby state. *Number the Stars* was based on another person's life and set in a country Lowry barely knew. Just before the publisher's deadline for her manuscript, she made a decision. She had to go to Denmark in order to visit places where the story was set. She traveled from the streets of Copenhagen to the shoreline where her protagonist Ellen Rosen escaped to Sweden. The author also incorporated authentic details. Danish scientists really did create a chemical to throw Nazi dogs off the scent when seeking escaping Jews. King Christian actually traveled alone; fellow Danes joked the whole country was his bodyguard. Lowry's trip helped to add authenticity to the book.

ANOTHER AWARD

Every year, the Association for Library Service to Children awards the Newbery Medal "to the author of the most distinguished contribution to American literature for children."[3] Named for eighteenth-century British bookseller John Newbery, the prize is a pinnacle for children's book authors. Books that win the award have its logo emblazoned on their covers—and their authors gain respect and increased sales. *Number the Stars* won the award in 1990, 13 years after Lowry's first novel was published. She was 52.

The year before, her son Grey had been married in a small German village, where his bride, Margaret, had grown up. In 1991, Lowry gave a speech about the book. Afterward, during the question and answer period, she recalled:

> A woman raises her hand. When the turn for her question comes, she sighs very loudly and says, "Why do we have to tell this Holocaust thing over and over? Is it really necessary?" I answer her as well as I can—quoting in fact, my German daughter-in-law, who has said to me, "No one knows better than we Germans that we must tell this again and again."[4]

The book proved that a familiar story can be retold in an unfamiliar way. The Newbery Medal did more than give Lowry the sort of critical acclaim and large audience of which most novelists can only dream; it made her more courageous than she had ever been as a writer. "I think the

1990 Newbery freed me to risk failure," she admitted a few years later.[5]

Her next gamble? Writing a novel so different from her previous work that her editor was not even sure how to edit it!

Above, students study The Giver, *Lowry's dystopian novel. Although controversial because many people believe the book's subject matter is inappropriate for young children, the novel is on many middle-school reading lists. Since its publication in 1993, it has sold almost 6 million copies.*

9

The Giver
Keeps on Giving

IN THE EARLY 1990s, Lois Lowry's parents were in their 80s and living at a nursing home in Charlottesville, Virginia. Physically frail, Lowry's mother was sharp as ever mentally. Her father was the opposite. He comfortably strolled with his daughter and flirted with nurses, but his memory was fading.

Lowry remembered in an interview,

My brother and I had prepared a photograph album filled with images to spark his memory. In 1956, he had a Green Chrysler that he loved. When he saw a picture of it, his eyes would always light up. That day he came upon a picture of two little girls, and he said, "There you are with your sister. I can't remember her name." I told him her name was Helen. He looked a little puzzled, a little confused and asked, "whatever happened to her?"[1]

Lowry explained how Helen died from cancer nearly 30 years before. He became very sad; to him, the loss was fresh. A few minutes later, he came across another photo of Helen. He asked what had happened to her.

A FALSE UTOPIA

Driving to the airport after visiting her father, Lowry thought about memory. She wondered if there was a way to make bad memories disappear like her father's sad recollections of Helen's death. She envisioned a society in which sad memories and even bad feelings and pain were permanently erased.

In a speech in Virginia, she said:

> And so, from the "what if," of my father's failing memory, and from my own musings about the compromises we make, I created a world—not a large one; a small community set in the future, in a time when technology had advanced in ways that would make human existence comfortable and safe through the manipulation of memory.
>
> But for me, because I write for a young audience, the questions that incite and inspire a book must always be presented through the consciousness of a young person. And so I created a boy, and I named him Jonas.[2]

It seemed ideal. As she developed the story, though, she realized that the world she was crafting was not a utopia. Utopias are idyllic worlds—worlds without war, hunger, or pain. Unfortunately it often takes an all-controlling, all-powerful government to eliminate pain and bad memories. The world she created was not a utopia but a *dystopia*, which the dictionary defines as "an imaginary place where people live dehumanized and often fearful lives." In these worlds, which are sometimes filled with poverty or starvation, people usually fear an all-controlling government that seeks to regulate every aspect of their citizens' lives. It does not matter how noble the government's intentions; eliminating everything considered bad usually means eliminating most of the good as well. This is often known as "the law of unintended consequences."

One of literature's most famous dystopias is depicted in Aldous Huxley's *Brave New World*. First published in 1932, this darkly satirical novel portrayed a society in which chemicals control every feeling and people are created to perform various jobs. The elite Alphas have the best careers and run the society. Physical maladies and even aging have been eliminated, but so has free will.

Author and philosopher Ayn Rand penned a similar novella in 1937, although it was not actually published until 1946. *Anthem* depicted a world in which individuality is outlawed and everyone is expected to work for the group. Free will does not exist—jobs are chosen by committee, and people assigned to them are expected to do the same work for the rest of their lives. *Anthem*, like Rand's other books, is a response to her fear that philosophies like communism and socialism might destroy free choice and individuality. She championed objectivism, an ethical theory that stated that an individual should not be prevented from pursing his or her dreams as long at this pursuit does not interfere with the dreams of others. *Anthem*'s author description notes: "Ayn Rand said that she decided to be a writer, not in order to save the world nor to serve her fellow men, but for the simple, personal, selfish, egotistical happiness of creating the kind of men and events she would like, respect and admire."[3]

Aldous Huxley

An illustration of Aldous Huxley, the English essayist and novelist best known for his dystopian novel, Brave New World, *which was published in 1932.*

Dystopia is also a common theme in film. Movies such as 1982's *Blade Runner* and 2002's *Minority Report*, both based on the works of science fiction author Philip K. Dick, dramatize the drastic choices a government takes to control crime at the expense of citizens' freedom.

Lowry told an interviewer,

> I began to play with the idea of people who had learned to manipulate memory. I realized such a story would have to be set in the future. I began creating a community quite different from the ones we now have. I never thought of the book as a science fiction novel or that I might need to explain its technology.[4]

WRITING *THE GIVER*

The world Lowry imagined became *The Giver*. Set in an unnamed time in the future, it depicted a society in which bad memories were erased, as were pain, prejudice, fear of death, and even hills and color. Told from the point of view of Jonas, an 11-year-old boy, the novel begins shortly before the Ceremony of Twelve, at which he will learn his Assignment. In Jonas's village, careers are chosen by the elders. From the age of 12, they begin job training; no one selects his or her own future.

Jonas is chosen to be the Receiver, the repository of the community's collective memory. It is an awesome responsibility. As he studies with the elderly Receiver that he will replace, the boy realizes how much his people have given up. His studies lead him to question the choices made by the elders, as well as those made by his parents.

At one point, Jonas asks the Receiver how often he advises the Committee of Elders, the community's rule-making organization. The man he now calls The Giver replies, "Sometimes I wish they'd ask for my wisdom more often—there are so many things I could tell them; things I wish they would change. But they don't want change. Life here is so orderly, so predictable—so painless. It's what they've chosen."[5]

Lowry was writing a book radically different than her other novels, far more different than even *Number the Stars*. It was a gamble, as she now had a faithful audience that might not want to take a chance on such a different book. It might even be categorized as science fiction, perhaps alienating loyal readers who were not interested in that genre.

Laboring over her first draft, Lowry understood her limitations. The publisher warned that the novel could not exceed 200 pages. If it did, they would have to charge more for it. Higher-priced books generally do not sell as well, and Lowry wanted to ensure that *The Giver* reached the largest possible audience.

She condensed a great deal of time into the last 20 pages so that the book would not exceed the limit. It is a decision she still regrets: "I think it was foolish of me to feel constrained by that at that time. Probably if I had mentioned it to my editor, he would have said, 'Make it as long as it needs to be.' I regret that, because I always felt that the last section of the book felt too rushed."[6]

Although Jonas's flight from the village and the travel afterward take up a decent period of time in the story, it is covered in less than two dozen pages. Fifteen years after writing the book, Lowry recalled:

> I feel as though that could have been explored in more depth
> and with more length. At the same time that I say that, though,
> I realize that for that period of time in the book I had the boy
> alone except for a baby so it would have been pretty hard to
> dream up things that would move plot along.[7]

It is a myth that most authors do not want anyone else to interfere with their "babies." Writers do not just send a manuscript to their publisher and expect that only grammatical errors and spelling mistakes will be corrected. No matter how successful they become, most novelists welcome feedback. Even Stephen King sends his manuscripts to a few trusted friends or colleagues who review it carefully.

Lowry remembers:

> In the summer of 1977, Steve called me and asked if I would be willing to read a manuscript of a book he was working on and he had a few questions about it that he wanted to ask me and I said, sure, and he sent me the manuscript and it was a manuscript for a book that was called *The Dead Zone*. I read it and I had a few questions and things I thought could be better done and I wrote a letter listing those things. In the manuscript he asked me questions in the margins, "does this work, should this happen sooner." I answered those in a letter, and since I didn't need the manuscript anymore I took it with all those questions on it and threw it away. Now what would that be worth today?[8]

After incorporating many of the suggestions made by the readers, the author sends it to the editor at his or her publishing house, who makes suggestions. Although the author revises throughout this process, he or she does not agree with every suggestion made. No one knows the book as well as the writer, and some ideas just do not work.

Walter Lorraine had been Lowry's editor since her first book and had been with Houghton Mifflin for almost 50 years. When he read the manuscript of *The Giver*, he knew the author was right: It was like nothing she had ever written before. Instead of editing the book alone, he gave the manuscript to two other editors. They read it and listed extensive notes, which they sent to Lowry.

"It was good, because it was a different book for me as well as for them and each of them raised questions that I needed to think about some more," Lowry admits. "I don't think the book would have been as successful if only he [Lorraine] had dealt with it. I think it was wise for him to turn it over to a couple of other people for their opinions, I think it served me well and it served the book well."[9] Lowry noted one significant change in a recent interview:

> In the original manuscript, the boy sees color for the first time in a red ball. One of the editors raised the question as to why this community would be manufacturing items with color when they have no color. I changed the object to an apple, and then when Jonas sees color it occurs in a natural object. In the end, I left most of the manuscript as it was, including the ambiguous conclusion.[10]

Changing the object from a ball to an apple injected a powerful symbol into the novel. Readers frequently find symbols in their favorite books, and these symbols often have religious references. In *Number the Stars*, the title came from Psalm 147, which Danish resistance fighter Peter reads as the group hides from the Nazis. The main character, Annemarie, notices the stars in the sky and hides her best friend Ellen's Star of David pendant, which identifies her as a Jew. Authors sometimes place symbols in their novels intentionally and sometimes they occur accidentally. In *The Giver*, it was a little bit of both.

The simple change of a ball to an apple heightened *The Giver's* religious theme. The forbidden fruit of knowledge that Adam and Eve eat in the Bible's Book of Genesis is often popularly depicted as an apple. When Eve eats the apple and then shares it with Adam, they gain knowledge but their newfound wisdom is costly. They are banished from paradise. Jonas first sees red in an apple, and he embarks on his own journey of knowledge. The wisdom he acquires leads to his escape from a village he once considered paradise.

"If [symbolism] is there," Stephen King advised in his book *On Writing,* "and if you notice it, I think you should bring it out as well as you can, polishing it until it shines and then cutting it the way a jeweler would cut a precious or semi-precious stone."[11]

CENSORSHIP

After another revision, Lowry submitted the manuscript. *The Giver* was published in 1993. Again, Lowry's gamble was rewarded. The symbols contributed to the book's success. It was even used by some churches as part of their curriculum.

"At the same time, some fundamentalist leaders want it removed from everyone's hands," Lowry admitted in a recent interview. "I am still, I must be honest, mystified by the challenges from the very conservative churches. I think, on one level, the book can be read supporting conservative ideals—it challenges the tendencies in any society to allow an invasive government to legislate lives."[12]

Lowry struggles to understand why a book she views as a celebration of freedom is so often challenged by parents and groups who want it pulled from their school libraries. "The book's been out there for fifteen years and over the course of that time I've watched it acquire a vast spectrum of audience of all sorts and the censorship had surprised me . . . it's been in the top ten challenged book in the US for years and years," Lowry says. There are those who find the scene of Jonas bathing an elderly woman objectionable, and others are upset by the murder of an infant by his father.

Lowry suspects that those criticisms are not only taken out of context but also provide cover for a greater, and to some parents, more objectionable issue. "I think what they're troubled by is a book that portrays a kid perceiving the hypocrisy of a well-ordered adult world and breaking rules in order to try and change that and I think that makes them uneasy, I'm guessing."[13]

Controversy usually helps a book's sales. Since its publication, *The Giver* has sold nearly 6 million copies worldwide. Besides being read in grades from elementary to high school, it has also appeared in a few masters theses by graduate students.

The book's message about the risks in a controlling government especially appealed to libertarians, who believe

Did you know...

Some of the rules depicted by *The Giver* have already been turned into laws. In the book's community, if a citizen breaks the rules three times he is "released." In 1994, the year after *The Giver*'s publication, California voters approved a "three strikes" law that mandated lengthy prison sentences for individuals convicted of a third felony. In the book, fire is not allowed in homes—there are no candles or fireplaces. In March 2008, the South Coast Air Quality Management District in California voted to make wood-burning fireplaces illegal in all new homes and remodels of existing homes by 2009.

that smaller government better serves all citizens. To them, the government should run only services that cannot be provided any other way, like military defense and border security, but other functions, such as social services and education, should be run privately.

CREATING A TRILOGY

In 1989, Lowry had taken a chance in writing a historical novel like *Number the Stars*. It won her a Newbery Medal. Only five years later, she took an even bigger gamble and was selected for her second Newbery. Rather than alienating her audience, *The Giver* brought her legions of new fans. She returned to the dystopian world she created in two more novels. In *Gathering Blue*, a young girl named Kira struggles in a village far less advanced technologically than the one portrayed in *The Giver,* yet readers learn that the story is set years later.

The main characters in *The Giver* and *Gathering Blue* meet in the final book in the trilogy, 2004's *The Messenger*. The novels were set in the future, following a scarcely described cataclysmic event. War had devastated cities, leaving them uninhabitable. Survivors from the ruins built their own societies, ones that did not rely on a central government, like the one in Washington, D.C. Instead, small communities crafted their own laws and punishments. The rural landscape created isolation and allowed them to exist with little outside interference.

The millennium was still new when attacks on the United States would so closely mirror those Lowry was describing in her trilogy that the author felt compelled to address the similarities in speeches to professional audiences and letters to school children. By then, however, Lowry was coping with her own terrible tragedy.

Above, Lois Lowry's son, Major Donald Grey Lowry Jr., in 1990. A pilot, Grey was killed when his plane crashed in 1995. The news of his death devastated his mother, who later published a testimony to her son in Looking Back, *her photo memoir.*

10

Sad Endings

TRAGEDY STRIKES AGAIN

And you know what, Thin Elderly? Sad parts are important. If I ever get to train a young dream-giver, that's one of the things I'll teach: that you must include the sad parts, because they are part of the story, and they have to be part of the dreams.[1]

—Apprentice dream-giver, Littlest One
to her teacher, Thin Elderly in *Gossamer*

THE CALL WOKE Lois Lowry in the middle of the night. It was the call every parent dreads. "Margaret, my daughter-in-law, was calling," Lowry remembered in her photo memoir, *Looking Back*. "In the bravest voice that I have ever heard, she

99

told me that Grey's plane had crashed and he had died. That was the saddest day of my life."[2]

Lowry flew to Germany, where the funeral was held. Her granddaughter was barely a toddler. During the funeral, there was a tiny interruption: The author was in the front row when she heard a murmur during the quiet service. Through open doors, a yellow butterfly entered. Looking behind her, she saw it hovering over the congregants. One of her last memories of her son was of him reading a book in German to his daughter. He taught her the word for butterfly: *schmetterling*.

Major Donald Grey Lowry Jr. was buried in 1995, his gravesite near the small German village where his wife had grown up. To his mother, the interruption of the butterfly felt like a message from her son. There was another. Lowry wrote:

> Because Grey was a pilot, everything he said in the plane was recorded. After his death, I was given a transcript of that recording, and so I know what my son's last words were. He was flying in formation, that day, with another plane. When Grey realized that something was wrong with his plane, he radioed the other pilot. "You're on your own," Grey said. Then he crashed and died.
>
> I think about those words a lot. They're a reminder. We're all on our own, aren't we? That's what it boils down to. We come into the world on our own . . . and leave it the same way. And between those times, we try to connect along the way with others who are also on their own.[3]

GREY'S REFLECTIONS

It was a difficult time, but Lowry possessed an amazing gift, for she could share her feelings not only with the words she wrote but in the speeches she gave. She spoke of connecting with others, especially young people. She described to audiences not only her emotions from the dribble of fan letters she received after her first novel was published, but also the way her son connected with someone on a drizzly British airfield.

Her son wrote a letter to his mother about the experience, a letter Lois Lowry gave to her own mother. It was in Katherine Hammersberg's things after she died, and Lowry read it at Grey's memorial service.

Grey Lowry had the first flight at an air show. After he landed, he made his way toward the VIP tent for coffee. His progress was interrupted by audience members who wanted him to sign their programs. From the corner of his eye, he noticed one eight-year-old boy hanging back shyly even as his parents tried to nudge him forward. "So I said to him, 'Would you like me to sign your program?' and he said, 'Oh please, sir,'" Lowry wrote in his letter. "And (although I'd been managing just fine, doing a juggling act, up till then), I said, "Would you mind holding my helmet for me while I sign my name?"

The boy took it. As Lowry signed the program, he glanced at the young fan. His attention was not on the pilot, but on his helmet. "He was stroking it as if it were made of the finest crystal. I was almost overwhelmed with the sudden awareness of what that helmet meant to him," Grey Lowry wrote, "what I symbolized to him . . . that I was a hero to that little boy, and to others like him."

Almost without realizing it, Lowry began to tell the boy that he had worn out his gloves on the flight and would need to get them replaced. Perhaps the boy wanted them? He did.

"And I gave him my perfectly good pair of gloves and said, 'Goodbye.' As I walked away, I thought, 'Lowry, you jerk, those were seventy-five dollar gloves.'" His irritation at himself faded, he explained in the letter, as every time he saw the boy, he was wearing the gloves, gloves that were "enormous on his little hands. And each time I saw him, I thought how lucky I was to have had that encounter with that child. I think most people go through their whole lives without ever having a moment like that, when they become aware of what they represent."[4]

At a speech six years later, Lois Lowry admitted:

> I think often about those seven seconds in which my son knew he was about to die. . . . What would his thoughts have been in that blurred, silent, frozen slice of time?
>
> I would like to think that it all came back to him then, and came together in a continuum: and that he could feel the hands that steadied him on his first bike; and his own child's hands when she reached out toward him and took her first steps; and the hands of the little boy who put on the enormous gloves that my son gave him as a gift.[5]

Greek playwright Aeschylus wrote, "He who learns must suffer, and even in our sleep, pain that cannot forget falls drop by drop upon the heart, and in our own despair, against our will, comes wisdom by the awful grace of God."[6] Words, even ones as profound as these, did not erase the pain of Grey's death, but Lowry was able to express her pride and love for her son in a photo memoir, *Looking Back,* which offered both 90-year-old pictures of her mother as well as testimony to Grey.

INTO THE PRESENT

By 2000, Lois Lowry's career epitomized that of a successful writer's. She maintained a summer home in New Hampshire and spent the rest of the year in a rambling Cambridge,

Massachusetts, home. When she was not at one of her two homes she was traveling—speaking at awards ceremonies and colleges, assisting theatrical companies with their versions of *The Giver*, and meeting Hollywood producers.

At the dawn of the twenty-first century, Lois Lowry was in her 60s, an age when many Americans retire. She never considered it. Why should she? She loved what she did and wrote nearly every day. The manual and electric typewriters were long gone. She had moved to a word processor when she wrote *The Giver* and shortly thereafter adopted a laptop for travels and a desktop at home. She wrote a chapter of *Gathering Blue* while awaiting a delayed flight in Knoxville, Tennessee.

She no longer even looks at printouts of her work. Instead, she revises as she goes along, fixing the previous chapters before starting on a new one.

> I am so comfortable with revision and correction on a computer . . . I had a writer friend visiting here once and she got up early in the morning and I glanced out from the upstairs window and she was seated at my backyard comfortably in a chair under a tree with a yellow legal pad working on a book

Did you know...

For more than 13 years, filmmakers have been trying to turn *The Giver* into a movie. Recently, director David Yates was attached to the project, but he dropped out because he was going to direct the last two Harry Potter movies.

she was writing, in longhand and I just can't imagine doing that—so everyone has their different methods.[7]

Now, when Lowry prints out a book, it's done—ready for the editors.

On September 11, 2001, four planes were hijacked and flown into the World Trade Center, in New York City; the Pentagon, outside Washington, D.C.; and a field in Pennsylvania (its flight toward Washington, D.C., is believed to have been aborted by the actions of passengers). The devastating attack would be compared to Pearl Harbor, and many believed that this day would also live in infamy. In just a few hours, nearly as many Americans died as at Pearl Harbor. Unlike that earlier attack, which had been on a military installation, the nearly 3,000 fatalities on September 11 were mainly civilians. The attack's impact was felt across the globe and radically altered everything from travel to foreign policy.

Just two months later, Lowry spoke in Ohio about how "in the aftermath of tragedy, I have read about movie productions halted and books-in-progress abandoned because their plots, once deemed simple 'thriller' and 'action,' suddenly were too ominous. I am uneasily aware that a book of mine, *Gathering Blue*, is set in a world that has turned savage and primitive after the collapse of organized civilization."[8]

In the aftermath of the attack, letters poured into the writer. Young fans wrote of course, but so did teachers and other adults. The fans often saw the similarities to real world events, and the adults wondered how they could protect children from witnessing the horrific images of the day.

Lowry believed that the power of words and books could overcome even the darkest terrors. In *The Giver*, most books were forbidden; the terrorists from September 11 represented a radical, repressive form of Islam that would eliminate novels like Lowry's. Even in the United States, some parents complained about her books: "Everything presented to kids should be positive and uplifting," one said.[9]

Reading that, Lowry recalled how her son Ben attended to his dying rabbit when he was eight. He put his pet in his bed and a pillow beneath his head, with the covers drawn up over his body. Later, he told his mother why, recalling the children's book *Charlotte's Web* and what he said was the "saddest sentence he had ever read": *No one was with her when she died.*

"There is nothing 'positive or uplifting' about a solitary death," Lowry said in a speech at the University of Richmond. "But there is something profoundly moving about a man, a gifted writer, E.B. White, who was able to put down on a page eight words . . . that went to the heart of a little boy and taught him something about loneliness and loss."[10]

Since then, Lowry has continued to write books that incorporate darker themes, including *The Messenger*, the concluding novel to the trilogy that began with *The Giver*. She also offered more humorous fiction such as *The Willoughbys*. Published in 2008, it is a parody of classic children's literature with siblings whose parents are trying to get rid of them even as their children are planning for the demise of their parents. She described herself on the book jacket as "a wizened, reclusive old woman who sits hunched over her desk thinking obsessively about the placement of commas."[11]

Lowry continues to embrace technology. Her Web site includes a blog so that fans can follow her travels and of course e-mail to send her questions. She even enjoys

A 1992 photo of Lowry with Martin Small, with whom she has had a relationship since 1979. In interviews, Lowry has praised Small's very positive influence on her writing.

Kindle, a device that holds books electronically—making reading lighter than carting books as carry-on luggage.

Even as she looks forward to the future, Lowry has not forgotten the past. In 2009, the short story that began it all, "Crow Call," will be published with illustrations.

Lois Lowry explained at a 1997 conference,

> I think children like—and need—happy endings, resolutions to the tangled and sometimes frightening journeys that they—

and we—and characters in books all make. They need to know that there are battles to be fought, and burdens to be carried; but that there are villages to return to, and new villages yet to be claimed. If Sam can return, so can they. If Jonas can find Elsewhere, and change the world that betrayed them, so can they.[12]

Real life ultimately is not a happy ending, but for Lois Lowry life still has its share of pleasures. In 1979, she began dating Martin Small, and the relationship continues to this day. "Martin and I have known each other since 1979, have lived together since 1980," Lowry noted. "I suppose a long and stable and happy relationship is always of benefit to one's work. Martin respects what I do, and gives me the privacy to do it with the solitude that writing requires. And he proofreads my manuscripts!"

The journeys taken by writers such as Lois Lowry offer a path for others: readers who want to follow the journeys of her characters and writers who hope to follow the journey of her work.

CHRONOLOGY

1937   Cena Ericson Hammersberg is born on March 20, 1937 in Honolulu, Hawaii. Her name is changed to Lois Ann a few weeks later.

1939–1942   The Hammersberg family moves to Brooklyn, New York. When her father leaves for military training and then the Pacific, the rest of the family moves to Pennsylvania.

1942–1948   She lives in Carlisle, Pennsylvania, where she attends Franklin Elementary School. Here, she begins to write stories and imagines being a writer.

1948–1950   The family moves to Tokyo during reconstruction, where her father is stationed.

1950–1951   Her father stays in Japan when family moves back to Pennsylvania. Lois begins high school.

1951–1952   The family moves to an army base at Governors Island, New York, where her father is stationed; she attends Curtis High School on Staten Island as a sophomore.

1952–1954   Lois transfers to a private school for girls, the Packer Collegiate Institute, in Brooklyn.

1954   She graduates from Packer Collegiate Institute and matriculates at Brown University.

1956–1958   After Lois marries naval officer Donald Grey Lowry, she drops out of Brown and moves to San Diego, California.

1958   Alix, the Lowrys' first daughter, is born while the couple is living in Connecticut.

1959   Their son Donald Grey, who is named for his father, is born in Florida.

1960–1963   When Lowry's husband begins studies at Harvard Law School, the family moves to Cambridge, Massachusetts.

1961   Their daughter Kristin is born.

1962   Their son Benjamin is born the same year Lois's sister, Helen, dies.

1963–1977 Lowry's husband graduates from Harvard Law School and the family moves to Portland, Maine.

1968 She enrolls at University of Southern Maine (USM) as an English major.

1972 She receives her BA from USM and enters graduate school. She also begins to sell nonfiction articles and textbooks.

1975 Her first published short story, "Crow Call," appears in *Redbook*.

1976 Her first novel, *A Summer to Die*, is sold.

1977–1979 *A Summer to Die* is published; she divorces Donald Grey Lowry and moves to Cape Porpoise, Maine.

1979 She moves to Boston, Massachusetts and begins to date Martin Small.

1980 Lowry's first series title, *Anastasia Krupnik*, is published.

1983 She buys summer home in New Hampshire.

1990 Lowry wins Newbery Medal for *Number the Stars.*

1993 She moves to Cambridge, Massachusetts, with Small.

1994 Lowry wins second Newbery for *The Giver.*

1995 Her son Donald Grey is killed in a plane crash.

1998 Lowry's photo memoir, *Looking Back*, is published.

2002 She moves from New Hampshire to Maine.

2008 Her novel *Gossamer* is performed as a play in Milwaukee, Wisconsin, and Portland, Oregon.

2009 Lowry's first published short story, "Crow Call," is released as an illustrated book.

NOTES

Chapter 1

1 Lois Lowry. "Wondering Where Everything Went." Speech to the National Council of English Teachers Annual Convention, Chicago, Ill. November 1996. http://www.loislowry.com/pdf/Wondering_Went.pdf.

2 Ibid.

3 Ibid.

4 "Epiphany." www.m-w.com. http://www.merriam-webster.com/dictionary/epiphany.

5 Joseph Campbell, *The Power of the Myth with Bill Moyers*. New York: Doubleday, 1988, p. 139.

6 Louis Lowry, *A Summer to Die*. New York: Delacorte Press, 1977, p. 10.

7 Campbell, *Power of the Myth*, p. 123.

Chapter 2

1 Lois Lowry, "Bright Streets and Dark Paths," lecture given at Brown University. March 4, 2001, p. 12.

2 John Bankston, interview with Lois Lowry, May 26, 2008.

3 Lowry, "Bright Streets," p. 10.

4 "A Date Which Will Live in Infamy: FDR Asks for a Declaration of War, December 8, 1941." History Matters: The U.S. Survey Course on the Web, George Mason University. http://historymatters.gmu.edu/d/5166/.

5 Bankston, interview with Lowry.

6 Lois Lowry, "The Remembered Gate and the Unopened Door," Sutherland Lecture, Chicago Public Library. May 4, 2001, p.15.

7 Lowry, "Bright Streets," pp. 11–12.

8 Ibid., p.13.

9 "Books." Loislowry.com. http://www.loislowry.com/books.html.

10 Lois Lowry, "The Beginning of Sadness," speech given at the Ohio Library Educational Media Association Annual Convention. November 2001, p. 9.

11 Lowry, "The Remembered Gate," p. 16.

12 Lowry, "Bright Streets," p. 4.

13 Lowry, "The Beginning," p. 9.

14 Bankston, interview with Lowry.

15 Lois Lowry, "The Village of Childhood," speech given at Children's Literature New England, Vermont. August 1997, p. 1.

16 Ibid.

17 Bankston, interview with Lowry.

18 Lowry, "Bright Streets," p. 6.

Chapter 3

1 Jack Kerouac, *On the Road*. New York: Viking Compass, 1959, pp. 5–6.

2 "About Brown." Brown University. http://www.brown.edu/web/about/history.

3 Lois Lowry, "Newbery Acceptance Speech," June 1994, p. 3.

4 Lois Lowry, "Bright Streets," p. 8.

5 Lois Lowry, "Wondering," http://www.loislowry.com/pdf/Wondering_Went.pdf.

6 Bankston, interview with Lowry.

7 Lowry, "Bright Streets," p. 7.

Chapter 4

1 Bankston, interview with Lowry.

2 Ibid.

3 Ibid.

4 Ibid.

5 Lois Lowry, "Bright Streets," pp. 18–19.

6 Lois Lowry, *Looking Back: A Book of Memories*. Boston: Houghton Mifflin, 2000, p. 125.

7 Bankston, interview with Lowry.

8 Ibid.

9 Ibid.

10 Ibid.

11 Lowry, "Bright Streets," p. 20.

12 Bankston, interview with Lowry.

13 Lowry, "Bright Streets," p. 22.

14 Bankston, interview with Lowry.

15 Lois Lowry, *Autumn Street*. Boston: Houghton Mifflin, 1980, p 1.

16 Lois Lowry, *Summer to Die*, p. 156.

17 Ibid., p. 156.

Chapter 5

1 S.E. Hinton, *The Outsiders*. New York: Penguin Putnam, 1967, p. 182.

2 Bankston, interview with Lowry.

3 "Frequently Asked Questions." Loislowry.com. http://www.loislowry.com/faq.html.

4 Ariel Gore, *How to Become a Famous Writer Before You're Dead: Your Words in Print and Your Name in Lights*. New York: Crown, 2007, p. 12.

5 Lowry, "Wondering," p. 5.

6 Ethel L. Heins, "Review of *Find a Stranger, Say Goodbye*," *The Horn Book Magazine*. June 1978, p. 258.

7 Lowry, "Wondering," p. 7.

8 Ibid., p. 8.

9 Lowry, "The Remembered Gate," p. 30.

Chapter 6

1 Lowry, "Wondering," p. 6.

2 Lois Lowry, "Village of Childhood," p. 9.

3 Lowry, "The Remembered Gate," p. 31.

4 Lowry, "Wondering," p. 13.

5 Lois Lowry, *Anastasia Krupnik*. Boston: Houghton Mifflin, 1979, p. 1.

6 Bankston, interview with Lowry.

7 Lowry, "Newbery Acceptance Speech," p. 6.

8 Ibid. p. 8.

Chapter 7

1 Lowry, "Bright Streets," pp. 15–19.

2 Ibid., p. 24.

3 Hinton, *The Outsiders*, p. 185.

4 Stephen King, *On Writing: A Memoir of the Craft*. Pocket Books: New York, 2000, p. 159.

5 Bankston, interview with Lowry.

6 Ibid.

Chapter 8

1 Lowry, "How Everything Turns Away," speech given at University of Richmond. March 2005, p. 6.

2 Anita Silvey, "Lois Lowry: The Edwards Award Winner Talks About *The Giver*, Interview." *School Library Journal* (June 2007), vol. 53, no. 6, p. 41.

3 "Newbery Medal Home Page." American Library Association: Association for Library Service to Children. http://www.pla.org/ala/alsc/awardsscholarships/literaryawds/newberymedal/newberymedal.cfm.

4 Lowry, "Newbery Acceptance Speech," pp. 4–5.

5 Ibid., p. 5.

Chapter 9

1 Silvey, "Lois Lowry," p. 38.

2 Lowry, "How Everything Turns Away," p. 13.

3 Ayn Rand, *Anthem*. New York: Pamphleteers, 1995, p. 107.

4 Silvey, "Lois Lowry," p. 39.

5 Lois Lowry, *The Giver*. Boston: Houghton Mifflin, 1993, p. 103.

6 Bankston, interview with Lowry.

7 Ibid.

8 Ibid.

9 Ibid.

10 Silvey, "Lois Lowry," p. 41.

11 King, *On Writing*, p. 198.

12 Silvey, "Lois Lowry," p. 40.

13 Bankston, interview with Lowry.

Chapter 10

1 Lois Lowry, *Gossamer*. Boston: Houghton Mifflin, 2006, p. 96.

2 Lowry, *Looking Back*, p. 170.

3 Ibid., p. 173.

4 Lowry, "Wondering," p. 15.

5 Lowry, "Bright Streets," pp. 30–31.

6 "Quotations by Author: Aeschylus." The Quotations Page. http://www.quotationspage.com/quotes/Aeschylus/.

7 Bankston, interview with Lowry.

8 Lowry, "Beginning of Sadness," p. 8.

9 Lowry, "How Everything Turns Away," pp. 8–9.

10 Ibid.

11 Lois Lowry, *The Willoughbys*. Boston: Houghton Mifflin, 2008, back jacket flap.

12 Lowry, "Village of Childhood," pp. 12–13.

WORKS BY LOIS LOWRY

1977 *A Summer to Die*

1978 *Find a Stranger, Say Goodbye*

1979 *Anastasia Krupnik*

1980 *Autumn Street*

1981 *Anastasia Again*

1982 *Anastasia at Your Service*

1983 *The One Hundredth Thing About Caroline; Taking Care of Terrific*

1984 *Anastasia, Ask Your Analyst; Us and Uncle Fraud*

1985 *Anastasia on Her Own; Switch Around*

1986 *Anastasia Has the Answers*

1987 *Rabble Starkey; Anastasia's Chosen Career*

1989 *Number the Stars; All About Sam*

1990 *Your Move, JP*

1991 *Anastasia at This Address*

1992 *Attaboy, Sam*

1993 *The Giver*

1995 *Anastasia Absolutely*

1996 *See You Around, Sam; Looking Back: A Book of Memories*

1997 *Stay! Keeper's Story*

1999 *Zooman*

2000 *Gathering Blue*

2003 *The Silent Boy*

2004 *The Messenger; Gooney Bird Greene*

2005 *Gooney Bird and the Room Mother*

2006 *Gossamer*

2007 *Gooney the Fabulous*

2008 *The Willoughbys*

POPULAR BOOKS

ALL ABOUT SAM

Fans wondered about Sam, Anastasia Krupnik's brother. Lowry wondered how to tell a story from a baby's point of view. In this, the first book in the series, the story starts as soon as he is born.

ANASTASIA KRUPNIK

Written to keep the author happy during a bleak winter, the first book in the series introduces Anastasia. Bright, silly, and prone to mood swings, she is discovering boys, notebooks, and great names for babies.

AUTUMN STREET

Although the details are fiction, much of the story is true. Elizabeth is six when her father leaves home during World War II and she moves with her older sister, baby brother, and mother to her grandparents' house in Pennsylvania.

GATHERING BLUE

In the middle book in *The Giver* trilogy, Kira is an orphan with a disability marked for death or banishment in her primitive village. Her skills with thread save her, as she is taken in by The Guardians, the powerful group that runs her community.

THE GIVER

Lowry's greatest critical and commercial success, this novel looks at a future world in which pain and prejudice have been erased at a price too high to imagine. Alternately dark and hopeful, it has inspired libertarians along with legions of young adults.

GOSSAMER

Describing the beings who give dreams and nightmares, this book looks at an older woman and the troubled eight-year-old she fosters. Lowry also co-wrote the play that debuted in 2008.

THE MESSENGER

The concluding book in *The Giver* trilogy follows the story of Matty, a young boy in *Gathering Blue*. Six years later, he is living in a peaceful village, one of the few who can safely enter the woods and deliver messages to other communities. Unfortunately, his village is changing as residents trade their values for things.

NUMBER THE STARS

Lowry's award-winning novel set in Denmark during World War II. The novel centers on a young girl named Annemarie and her family, who risk their lives to protect a young Jewish girl, Ellen Rosen, from the Nazis.

A SUMMER TO DIE

In the author's debut novel, Meg explores her love of photography and deals with the loss of her older sister, Molly.

THE WILLOUGHBYS

The Willoughbys are a nice, old-fashioned family just like all the nice, old-fashioned families in nice, old-fashioned children's books. Well, except for the fact that the parents are hoping to sell the house while on vacation, leaving their four children homeless. The children then plot their parents' demise. Other than that, it's a very traditional children's book.

POPULAR CHARACTERS

ANASTASIA KRUPNIK

Anastasia has hair the color of Hubbard squash, 14 freckles across her nose (and 7 others in places she preferred people not to know about). She also has notebooks, an ever-changing list of hates and loves, and two rather odd parents.

ANNEMARIE JOHANSEN

The main character of *Number the Stars*, Annemarie is a young girl during World War II who becomes part of the Danish Resistance when her family hides her best friend, Ellen Rosen, from the Nazis.

GOONEY BIRD

Gooney is an unusual second grader in Lowry's latest series.

JONAS

Jonas is about to find out his entire future. At the Ceremony of Twelve, he learns that he will be The Receiver, the repository of all the memories for his community. The knowledge, however, comes at a high price.

KIRA

Kira's disability could cost her life. After her mother dies, the nine-year old faces an uncertain future. Protected by The Guardians, she learns that their generosity masks horrible secrets.

SAM KRUPNIK

Sam was born on the pages of the Anastasia books, but his own novels were given life by the fans. They wanted to know more about the little mischievous boy. In the Sam books, they find out.

MAJOR AWARDS

1978 *A Summer to Die* wins the International Reading Association's Children's Book Award.

1981 *A Summer to Die* is awarded the California Young Reader Medal for Young Adult Fiction.

1987 *Rabble Starkey* is given the Boston Globe-Horn Book Award for fiction.

1991 *Number the Stars* wins the Dorothy Canfield Fisher Children's Book Award.

1990 *Number the Stars* is selected for the Newbery Medal and the National Jewish Book Award.

1991 *All About Sam* is given the Mark Twain Award.

1994 *The Giver* is selected for the Newbery Medal.

1998 Lowry receives the Educational Paperback Association Jeremiah Ludington Memorial Award.

2007 Lowry wins the Margaret A. Edwards Award for lifetime achievement from the American Library Association.

BIBLIOGRAPHY

Books

Campbell, Joseph, and Bill Moyers. *The Power of Myth*. New York: Doubleday, 1988.

Gore, Ariel. *How to Become a Famous Writer Before You're Dead: Your Words in Print and Your Name in Lights*. New York: Crown, 2007.

Hinton, S.E. *The Outsiders*. New York: Penguin Putnam, 1967.

"Lois Lowry," in *Authors and Artists for Young Adults*. Vol. 32. Detroit: Gale Group, 2000.

"Lois Lowry," in *Major Authors and Illustrators for Children and Young Adults*, 2nd ed., 8 Vols. Detroit: Thomson/Gale, 2002.

"Lois Lowry," in *St. James Guide to Young Adult Writers*, 2nd ed. Detroit: St. James Press, 1999.

Lowry, Lois. *Looking Back: A Book of Memories*. Boston: Houghton Mifflin, 1998.

Kerouac, Jack. *On the Road*. New York: Viking Compass, 1959.

King, Stephen. *On Writing: A Memoir of the Craft*. New York: Pocket Books, 2000.

Markham, Lois. *Lois Lowry: Meet the Author*. Santa Barbara: Learning Works, 1995.

Periodicals

Anderson, Stuart. "The Books that Rock the Cradle: Libertarian Themes in Children's Fiction," *Reason* Vol. 37, no. 8 (Jan 2006): p. 52(5).

Heins, Ethel L. "Review of *Find a Stranger, Say Goodbye*," *Horn Book Magazine* (June 1978): p. 258.

Silvey, Anita. "Lois Lowry: The Edwards Award Winner Talks About *The Giver*," *School Library Journal* Vol. 53 no. 6 (June 2007): p. 41.

Speeches

Transcripts from speeches given by Lois Lowry that are cited in this book can be found at http://www.loislowry.com/speeches.html.

Lowry, Lois. "The Beginning of Sadness," Ohio Library Educational Media Association Annual Convention, Loislowry.com. Available online. URL: http://www.loislowry.com/pdf/Beginning_of_Sadness.pdf.

———. "Bright Streets and Dark Paths," Brown University, Loislowry.com. Available online. URL: http://www.loislowry.com/pdf/Bright_Streets.pdf.

———. "Newbery Acceptance Speech," Loislowry.com. Available online. URL: http://www.loislowry.com/pdf/Newbery_Award.pdf.

———. "The Remembered Gate and the Unopened Door," Sutherland Lecture, Loislowry.com. Available online. URL: http://www.loislowry.com/pdf/Remembered_Gate.pdf.

———. "The Village of Childhood," Children's Literature New England, Loislowry.com. Available online. URL: http://www.loislowry.com/pdf/Village_Childhood.pdf.

———. "Wondering Where Everything Went," National Council of Teachers of English, Loislowry.com. Available online. URL: http://www.loislowry.com/pdf/Wondering_Went.pdf.

Other Sources

"Adolf Hitler," BBC: Historic Figures. Available online. URL: http://www.bbc.co.uk/history/historic_figures/hitler_adolf.shtml.

Brown University. Available online. URL: http://www.brown.edu/.

"A Date Which Will Live in Infamy: FDR Asks for a Declaration of War," History Matter: The U.S. Survey Course on the Web, George Mason University. Available online. URL: http://www.historymatters.gmu.edu/d/5166/.

"History of Brown," Brown University. Available online. URL: http://www.brown.edu/web/about/history.

Lois Lowry. Available online. URL: http://www.loislowry.com.

"Lois Lowry," Educational Paperback Association's Top 100 Authors. Available online. URL: http://www.edupaperback.org/showauth.cfm?authid=62.

BIBLIOGRAPHY

"Lois Lowry," Houghton Mifflin: Trade and Reference Division. Available online. URL: http://www.houghtonmifflinbooks. com/catalog/authordetail.cfm?authorID=260.

"World War II," BBC. Available online. URL: http://www.bbc. co.uk/topics/world_war_2.

FURTHER READING

Gore, Ariel. *How to Become a Famous Writer Before You're Dead: Your Words in Print and Your Name in Lights*. New York: Crown, 2007.

Huxley, Aldous. *Brave New World*. Cutchogue, New York: Buccaneer Books, 1932.

King, Stephen. *On Writing: A Memoir of the Craft*. New York: Pocket Books, 2000.

Rand, Ayn. *Anthem*. New York: Pamphleteers, 1946.

PICTURE CREDITS

INDEX

ABOUT THE CONTRIBUTOR

The author of more than four-dozen biographies for young adults, including books about Stephen Hawking, Margaret Mead, and F. Scott Fitzgerald, **JOHN BANKSTON** lives in Newport Beach, California. As a teenager, he spent his summers in Kennebunkport, Maine, not far from where Lois Lowry began her writing career. He has worked as an actor, a screenwriter, and a legal assistant. He is currently revising a young adult novel, *18 to Look Younger*. John Bankston does all his first drafts in longhand on college ruled notebook paper.